Leonardo DiCaprio
Romantic Hero

Leonardo DiCaprio
Romantic Hero

BY MARK BEGO

A JOHN BOSWELL ASSOCIATES BOOK

**Andrews McMeel
Publishing**

Kansas City

www.andrewsmcmeel.com

Library of Congress Cataloging-in-Publication Data on file
ISBN: 0-8362-6972-1

Cover and book design by Charles Kreloff

ATTENTION SCHOOLS AND BUSINESSES
Andrews McMeel books are available at quantity discounts with bulk purchase for educational, business, or sales promotional use. For information, please write to: Special Sales Department, Andrews McMeel Publishing, 4520 Main Street, Kansas City, Missouri 64111.

DEDICATIONS

To Gillian Boswell and the fourth grade class at The Hewitt School.

—JBA

To one of my dearest and most outrageous friends, Angela Bowie
Libras rule, baby . . . don't you ever forget it!
—MB

ACKNOWLEDGMENTS

The author would like to thank the following people for their assistance in the research and production of this book:

Robert Bennett (my film watching buddy!)
John Boswell
Patty Brown
Euvona Eatman
A. J. Flick
Glenn Hughes
Sindi Markoff Kaplan
Charles Kreloff
Virginia Lohle, and Rich and Ken at
    Star File Photos
Marie Morreale (you're the best!!!)
Photofest Photos
Ruffa & Ruffa
Sygma Photos
. . . and of course, Bob and Mary Bego

PHOTO CREDITS:

page 5, Frank Trapper/Sygma; **pages 10 & 14**, Darlene Hammond/Archive Photos; **pages 11, 18, & 22**, Gwendolen Cates/Sygma; **pages 12,13,15,16,17 & 21**, Lester Sloan/Gamma Liaison; **pages 19 & 32** Gregory Pace/Sygma; **page 20**, Kelly Jordan/Sygma; **pages 23,30,38,40,41,42 & 80**, Vincent Zuffante/Star File Photos; **pages 31 & 33**, Jimmy Gaston/FSP/Gamma Liason; **page 39**, Jeffrey Mayer/Star File Photos; **page 41**, Mike Guastella/Star File Photos; **page 41**, Barry King/Gamma; **pages 41 & 85**, Patrick McMullen/Liaison; **page 41**, Benainous/Duclos/Gamma Liason; **page 63**, Clasos Press/Gamma Liason; **page 82**, Fred Prouser/Reuters/Archive Photos; **page 83**, Sam Mircovich/Reuters/Archive Photos; **page 84**, Tim Graham/Sygma; **page 88 & 89**, Oscar Abolafia/Gamma Liason; images on **pages 26 & 55** from the video edition of *Critters 3,* New Line Home Video/Turner Home Entertainment; images on **pages 55, 56 & 60** from the video edition of *Total Eclipse,* New Line Home Video/Turner Home Entertainment; all other images courtesy of Photofest.

Front cover photo: Photofest
Back cover photos: Gene Shaw/Star File Photos; Clasos Press/Gamma Liason; and Photofest

Contents

What Makes Leonardo DiCaprio Tick? *6*

Leo's Childhood *10*

This Boy's Life *24*

What's Eating Leo DiCaprio? *30*

Leonardo Scores *42*

Twentieth-Century Romeo *56*

Titanic—An Epic Role *70*

Unmasking Leo's Talent *80*

Filmography *90*

Educational Films *95*

Television Shows *95*

What Makes Leonardo DiCaprio Tick?

He's young, sexy, blond and handsome. He has piercing blue eyes, boyish good looks, and a mischievous smile. In his brief but explosively eventful acting career, he has been a regular cast member on two network television series and has climbed to the top of his fame in the span of eleven feature films. Like dozens of child actors in Hollywood, he began his experience in front of the cameras doing television commercials, and facing show business rejection in countless casting calls and auditions. However, once his career started to take off, there was no stopping him.

In 1993 he made his mainstream film debut in *This Boy's Life* opposite such heavyweight stars as Robert DeNiro and Ellen Barkin. By the time he was nineteen, he had his first Academy Award nomination for his heartfelt portrayal of mentally handicapped Arnie in the quirky hit *What's Eating Gilbert Grape?* Since that time he has starred as a modern-day Romeo in the sizzling screen adaptation of *William Shakespeare's Romeo + Juliet*, portrayed drug-addicted street poet Jim Carroll in *The Basketball Diaries*, played a cocky young gunslinger in *The Quick and the Dead*, and acted comically maladjusted Hank opposite Meryl Streep in *Marvin's Room*. Now, in 1998, as

Leonardo DiCaprio and Kate on the bow of the *Titanic*.

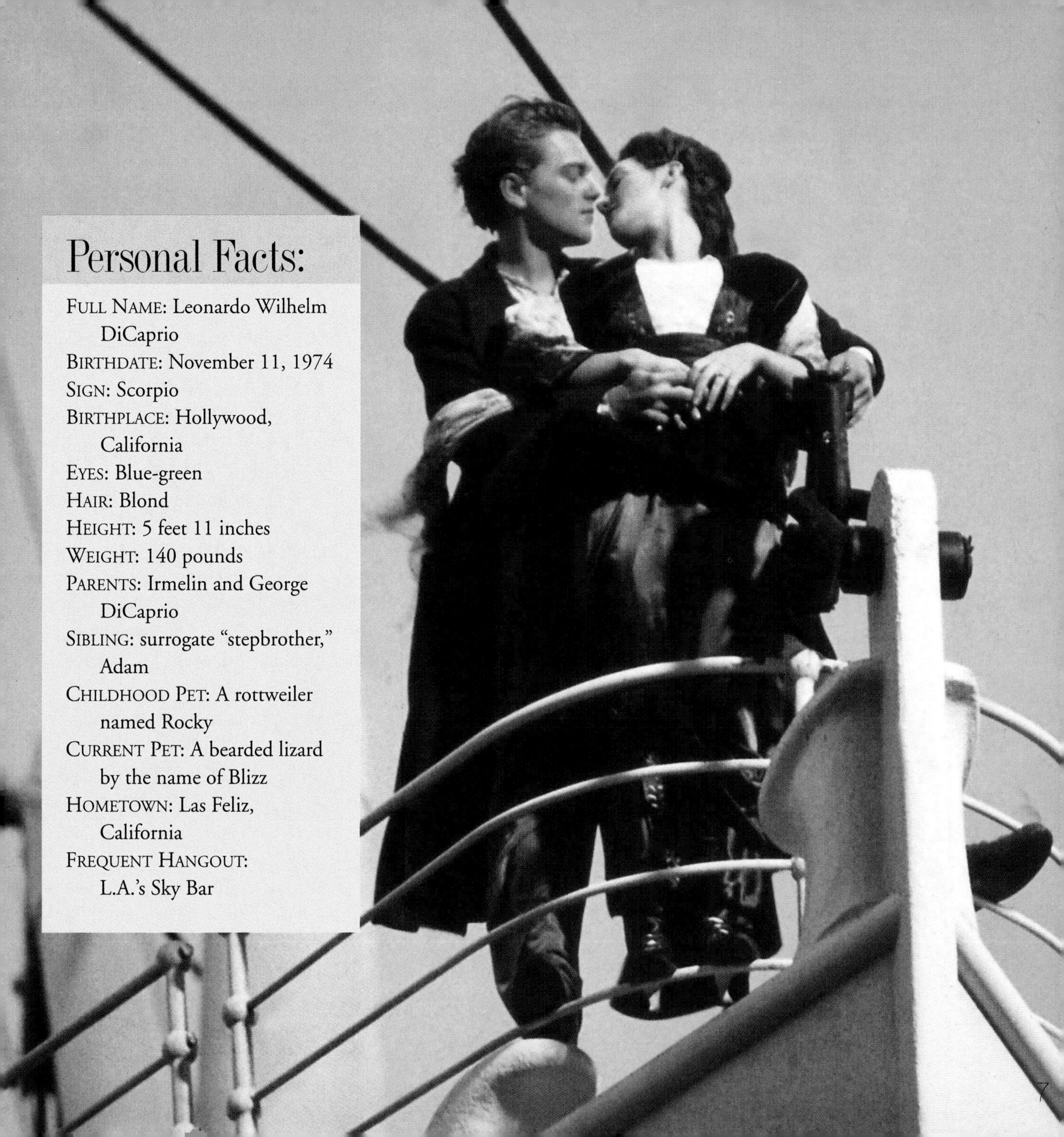

Personal Facts:

FULL NAME: Leonardo Wilhelm
DiCaprio
BIRTHDATE: November 11, 1974
SIGN: Scorpio
BIRTHPLACE: Hollywood,
California
EYES: Blue-green
HAIR: Blond
HEIGHT: 5 feet 11 inches
WEIGHT: 140 pounds
PARENTS: Irmelin and George
DiCaprio
SIBLING: surrogate "stepbrother,"
Adam
CHILDHOOD PET: A rottweiler
named Rocky
CURRENT PET: A bearded lizard
by the name of Blizz
HOMETOWN: Las Feliz,
California
FREQUENT HANGOUT:
L.A.'s Sky Bar

Romantic hero Leo with Claire Danes in *William Shakespeare's Romeo + Juliet.*

He still prefers quirky roles in offbeat films to making more obvious choices.

the leading man in what is being heralded as the biggest international blockbuster film of the century—*Titanic*—there is nowhere you can go on the planet where someone doesn't know the name of Leonardo DiCaprio!

At the age of 23, how many young actors in Hollywood can reflect on the last ten years of their life and claim such a breathtaking list of credits? There aren't many young film stars today who can look back upon their careers and see such a brilliant blend of commercial acclaim and artistic success. Leonardo DiCaprio is one such rare animal, in a jungle of mere actors.

In addition to his adventurous choices in film roles, Leo, as his friends call him, has also gained a headline-grabbing reputation for all-night partying and some wild behavior. He simply looks upon it as a character developing exercise. According to him, "I've always been wild. Now I have a lot more material to work with."

Although he grew up in Hollywood, California, he came from the seedier side of the tracks, and was far from being an overprivileged rich kid. He came from modest beginnings, and he is proud of what he has

Leo and Kate in *Titanic* in a love affair against time and against fate.

accomplished with his acting career. "The best thing about acting," he proclaims, "is that I get to lose myself in another character and actually get paid for it. It's a great outlet. As for myself, I'm not sure who I am. It seems that I change every day."

While he is truly basking in the acclaim that is being heaped upon him from *Titanic*, this does not signal his entry into a future filled with big blockbuster commercial films. He still prefers quirky roles in offbeat films to making more obvious choices. In fact, he insists

that he wants to avoid "having my face everywhere. Basically, I only want to trust my instincts with everything I choose. I want to go with things that have integrity and that I feel I'm doing for me."

There was a point during the casting of *Titanic* in which director James Cameron wasn't sure that Leo was right for the role of Jack. There was also a point in which DiCaprio himself was skeptical about portraying the part altogether. What was it that finally convinced Leonardo that the role of Jack was

right for him? And what was it like to film such a physically demanding role?

The choices that he has made so far have taken him down many unexpected paths. What is his unique and sometimes unconventional relationship with his parents? What is it that has always driven him to choose the most unlikely paths in life and how has he made them work to his advantage? How is he able to totally immerse himself in a film role? And, better yet, what is it that makes Leonardo DiCaprio tick?

Leo's Childhood

As an aspiring actor, the first time Leonardo saw himself on the screen was in the 1980s' revival of the TV series *Lassie*.

I n the Hollywood acting community, Leonardo DiCaprio is a very unique individual—as an actor, as a person, and as the hottest young male star of the moment. It all stems back to the way he was raised. His perspective, his drive, his conviction, and his integrity can be traced to his childhood.

Many people in their late teens and early twenties think that their parents are very square and unhip, so much so that they can't wait until they are old enough to move out of the house and out on their own. Not Leonardo DiCaprio. He's the exact opposite. In fact,

Leo's Favorite Things

FAVORITE ACTORS:
Jack Nicholson, River Phoenix

FAVORITE COLORS: Dark
Green, also Purple and Black

FAVORITE FOOD: Pasta

FAVORITE FAST FOOD: Burritos

FAVORITE BOOKS: *Lord of the Flies* and *A Raisin in the Sun*

FAVORITE CLOTHES: Thrift
shop clothes, baggy jeans, T-
shirts, flannel shirts, Doc
Martens shoes

FAVORITE MUSIC: Reggae, Rap

FAVORITE BAND: Pink Floyd

HOBBIES: Making home videos

FAVORITE TV SHOW:
Twilight Zone reruns

CHILDHOOD COLLECTIONS:
Baseball Cards, Fossils

Leonardo and his mother, Irmelin, in the early 1990s.

he just recently moved out on his own. For years he lived with his mother in the Las Feliz section of Los Angeles, not far from his father's home.

"My parents are so a part of my life," Leo explains, "that they're like my legs or something. . . . And it wasn't like they created a false good time—that they went out of their way to show me fabulous things. It was just that they were around and they were great."

His mother, Irmelin, is a pretty blonde woman born in Germany. His father, George, is an eccentric ex-hippie. Although they are both still legally married to each other, they have been separated for years. Their relationship still intersects on their star son, Leonardo, because they both work for his production company. His mother handles his scheduling, and his father screens the dozens and dozens of scripts that are sent in for his consideration.

Although George has been living for several years with Peggy Ferrar, an exercise physiologist, his relationship with Irmelin has always remained friendly. It is an unconventional family unit, but somehow it works and everyone is happy with it. Leonardo is also very close to Peggy and his maternal grandmother, Helena, known to everyone as Oma.

Explaining his parents' backgrounds, Leo says, "My mom came to this country from Germany when she was very young. She met my dad in college. They moved out to L.A. because they heard it was such a great place and then my mom became pregnant. They moved right into the heart of Hollywood, because they figured that's where all the great stuff was going on in this great town. Meanwhile, it was the most disgusting place to be."

When Irmelin was pregnant with Leo, she and George took a trip to Europe. They were standing in the Uffuzi Museum looking at an exhibit when Irmelin felt Leonardo give her a hard kick from within. She just happened to be looking at a painting by Leonardo da Vinci at that exact moment, and she viewed it as a psychic connection with her unborn child. She knew right then and there what she was going to name him. On November 11, 1974, she gave birth to Leonardo Wilhelm DiCaprio, destined to be a creative soul of his own unique design.

His father, George DiCaprio, still sports shoulder-length hair and was a true nonconformist from early on. For years he made his living distributing underground comic books to newsstands and avant-garde smoke shops. He also hung out with a very unconventional group of liberal thinkers.

Abbie Hoffman's son, America, was one of Leonardo's friends when he was growing up. Visitors to the DiCaprio household included alcoholic poet Charles Bukowski and comic book legends like Harvey Peker and R. Crumb.

According to George, "Leonardo got a very alternative look at things early on . . . [he was] never excluded from conversations about sex or drugs."

Leo is thankful for all of the experiences he had as a child. They helped to shape him into the well-rounded person that he is today. According to him, "I think what I liked best about my childhood was the repetitiveness of the things we did. I think when you're a kid, and you do a whole bunch of things, see a thousand different things, it's all a blur and you really don't remember anything. But we did the same things—went to the same museums, took the same pony rides—and those things have become locked in my memory as one good experience."

Although his parents separated not long after he was born, Leonardo recalls always being very close to both of them. "I grew up in Hollywood," he explains, "but not in any rich neighborhood. But my parents, who were split up, were so good at keeping my environment strong and keeping everything around me not focused on the fact

Leonardo and his grandparents, Helena and Wilhelm.

His first acting assignments were as the star of dozens of TV commercials.

L.A. for a while now. I'd go on trips with him to all the comic book stores around town when I was little."

A creative and curious boy, even from an early age, Leonardo remembers nothing but fun times with his parents, whether he was staying with his mother or with his father, Peggy, and Peggy's son, Adam. "I owe so much to my parents and the way I was brought up, but I have sometimes overlooked it—and it's something that I don't want to overlook. The things that you did with them—whether it was spending every Sunday morning with your dad and eating French toast and watching *Popeye*, or decorating the Christmas tree with your mother—these are the memories that help you be happy," he warmly recounts.

Although Hollywood, California, seems like a wonderful, affluent, magical place to grow up, there are also some very seedy

sections and lots of harsh realities that are very evident. Leonardo was not raised in the lap of luxury. In fact, he claims, "We were in the poorhouse. I would walk to my playground and see, like, a guy open up his trench coat with a thousand syringes. I saw some major homosexual activity outside my friend's balcony when I was five. To this day it's an imprint on my mind."

However, being in Hollywood, the center of the show business world, also presented some fascinating creative possibilities. A hyperactive child who liked to entertain people, Leonardo displayed acting talents from a very early age. "I always wanted to become an actor," he says. "My parents knew I was outgoing as a child, and whatever people came over I'd automatically do impressions of them as soon as they left; it was my mom's favorite thing."

Leonardo watched with fascination when Adam was cast in a

that we were poor. They got me culture. They took me to museums. They showed art to me. They read to me. And my mother drove two hours a day to take me to University Elementary School. My father picked me up. He'd been an underground comic artist in New York in the 60's and he's been distributing comics and records and books in

Golden Grahams breakfast cereal TV commercial. Recalls Leonardo, "I asked my dad how much Adam made from it. He said, 'About $50,000.' Fifty thousand dollars! It just kept going through my head: My brother has $50,000! And that kept being my driving force. I just remember for, like, five years thinking my brother was better than me because he had that." Watching Adam accomplish this had a lasting impression on him. It made him realize what kind of possibilities existed in his own hometown. It wasn't long before he was convinced that he wanted to get into show business as well.

"My love of performing goes way back," DiCaprio recalls. "My mom got me on *Romper Room* when I was five—it was my favorite [TV] show. But they couldn't control me. I would run up and smack the camera, and I'd jump around and do my little flips and routines. I wish I could get that tape now. But I have other memories, too."

When Adam landed a recurring role in a big network television series, Leonardo was green with envy. As he explains it, "My stepbrother was [an actor] for many many many years. He

He claims that his Hollywood childhood was far from glamorous.

A boy and his dog.

was on *Battlestar Gallactica*, a short-lived series. He inspired me. He would come home every day: 'I shot this . . . ' Jealousy there! That inspired me to get into it. I have been wanting to do that for like five years."

However, it wasn't long before young Leonardo ended up getting into acting as well. "My mom's friend worked at Harry Gold [talent agency]," he recalls. "She said I would be good for acting. So, I went in and did this [reading], and they said I was good. I started to go on auditions. It took me about a year." However, Leonardo was not an overnight success. The first lesson he learned in the acting realm was that of rejection.

Leonardo recalls one such episode when he was ten years old. There were a lot of other little boys at the audition as well. One by one the woman who was doing the casting would survey each of them and announce, "Not him, not him, not him. You two stay." When she looked at Leo, she pointed her finger and declared, "Not him." He was crushed. According to him, "I was heartbroken. I went up to her and asked why she hadn't picked me. 'Wrong haircut,' she said."

"On the way home in the car," he continued, "I cried and said, 'Dad, I really want to become an actor, but if this is what it's about I don't want to do it.' He put his arm around me and said, 'Someday, Leonardo, it will happen for you. Remember these words. Just relax.' And then I stopped crying, and I said, 'O.K.'"

Meanwhile, his childhood surroundings remained less than glamorous. In 1995, when he was interviewed by *The New York Times*, Leonardo took writer Jesse Green on a tour of his growing up hangouts. Pointing out different places in Hollywood, Leonardo narrated, "Here's where I lived from 11 to 15 [years old]. There's my old basketball net. And there's where I used to get on the roof and throw avocados at people." The tour continued with: "That Thrifty store used to be a Ralph's [supermarket]—I stole my first piece of bubble gum there, but I stopped because I believe in karma. This abandoned lot is where I used to play with car parts and get beat up."

Finally, his first break in the business came. Leonardo's initial experience in front of the cameras for a national TV commercial came

Up on the roof in Hollywood, California.

In school, Leonardo was always the class clown.

A hyperactive child who liked to entertain people, he displayed acting talents from a very early age.

when he was fourteen years old. It was for Matchbox toy cars and trucks.

Although he had landed his first television job, when it was over, it was back to the cattle call auditions to find his next opportunity. It is a competitive business, where every agent and casting director has their own idea as to what will sell. He recounts, "Another lady took me on and changed my name. Leonardo DiCaprio was 'too ethnic.' I got changed into something more white bread, so I could go to auditions and say, 'Look, I'm Lenny Williams and I have blond hair.'"

A cute, hyperactive young boy, it wasn't long before Leo landed more work—using his own name. Educational films, including the Disney-produced *Mickey's Safety Club* and *How to Deal With a Parent Who Takes Drugs*, gave him further experience.

Next came guest appearances on various television series. He vividly recalls the first time he saw himself on television. According to him, "I did two episodes of *Lassie*. I remember just being all excited." After that came additional roles on other series including *Roseanne* and

The Outsiders. On the TV soap opera *Santa Barbara,* Leo portrayed the part of a teenage alcoholic.

Amidst all of this activity came his first girlfriend and his first disastrous date experience. As he explains it, "My most devastating girlfriend was in junior high. We were totally in love, and we finally went out on a date to see *When Harry Met Sally . . .* I was so uncomfortable. I remember her eating this French-dip sandwich and the only thing I knew how to do was make fun of her and she got all freaked out. She didn't talk to me for a long time. Every two weeks she had library study, and I'd ditch class 'cause that's the only place where I knew she'd be. Her name was Sessie. Sexy Sessie. It sucked!"

Although his romantic life was fizzling, his career was soaring. He recalls, "Then I finally went to [TV series] *Parenthood.* I was like really excited about it. I had seen the movie lots of times. I knew what the character was like, and knew I would be good at it. I tried out for it, and then I went on a callback. I was one of the final three. I really concentrated. I went in there and did my best, and I got the part."

It wasn't long before he learned

His film career started with an appearance in a TV commercial for Matchbox model cars and trucks.

Even from the very beginning, Leonardo had the chiseled look of a star.

that success on television can be short-lived at best. He explains, "My first TV show had been *Parenthood*, which got canceled after thirteen episodes. I played Garry Buckman, the kid who masturbated and was really disturbed that his father left."

Leonardo was already sharpening his skills at playing misfits in front of the camera. According to him at the time, "I haven't played a cheerful boy yet. But emotionally ill characters like Garry give me a chance to really act."

When he wasn't acting, he kept busy hanging out with his friends, and devoted time to collecting basketball and baseball cards. While growing up, the schools that Leonardo attended included The Center for Enriched Studies and John Marshall High School, both in Los Angeles. However, he didn't enjoy school much, and once he got his first taste of acting, he found it difficult to get interested in studying things out of books. He concentrated instead on becoming the class clown.

"I was frustrated in school," he confesses. "I wasn't happy learning things. I know it's up to you to a degree, but a lot of times school is

It wasn't long before young Leonardo had his sights on big things for his career.

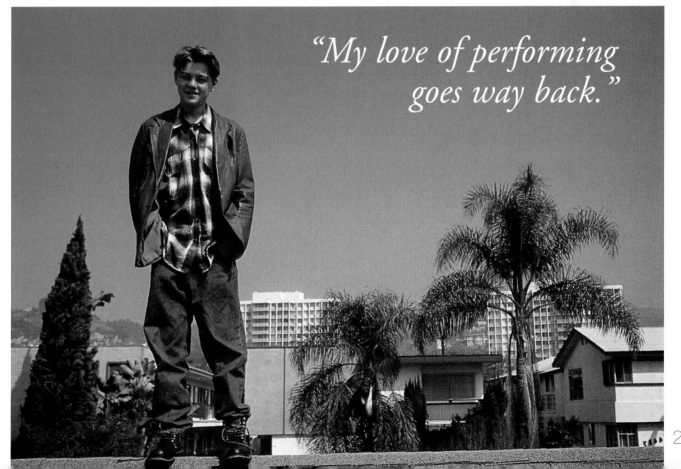

"*My love of performing goes way back.*"

just so dull and boring, it's hard for a kid to learn in that environment. You go to school, you go to this class, study this, study that, get your homework, go home. There's hardly any vibrance there. I could never focus on things I didn't want to learn. I used to do break-dancing skits with my friend at lunchtime. I had this one science class where the teacher would give me ten minutes after the class ended and I would get up and do improv. I needed to go to a place where I was excited about what I was learning. For me, it's all about getting a person interested in a subject by linking a lot of happiness to it, a lot of joy in doing it. That was lacking for me—and maybe a lot of other kids in this country."

He was becoming a bit of a misfit in his classes. On one particular occasion, Leonardo alarmed his teachers and the school officials when he drew a swastika on his forehead, as part of his improvised imitation of mass murderer Charles Manson. His parents, however, merely shrugged their shoulders, chalking it up to harmless adolescent rebellion. Thankfully, his acting career rescued him from having to conform to mundane school rules.

His next on-camera assignment came in 1991, when he was cast in a regular role on TV's *Growing Pains*. Leonardo played Luke, the homeless boy. One of the unique aspects of filming the show *Growing Pains* was that he was allowed to take a break from attending classes, as he qualified for a special home study program.

Another new aspect about working on *Growing Pains* was the fact that it was filmed in front of a live studio audience, very much like performing in a play. Leonardo explained what his typical week was like while working on the show: "Monday, we come in and do a cold reading. We just read our scripts around the table, then we go in, and we start moving around with the script, on the sets, then we read with our script. Then the next day we are working on the set, rehearsing with our sides [individual script pages]. By the third day we should have it memorized, all of our lines. We block everything: where we are going to move, then we practice all day before showtime. On Thursday, we actually tape on Thursday, just in case there is a mess-up. It is pretty fun. More fun than filming every day. The hardest part is when the curtain goes up, and you're really nervous."

Leonardo's tenure on *Growing Pains* was, however, brief, as the series was canceled following the season he appeared on the program. Although this could be viewed as a negative thing, it was a matter of perfect timing. Through all of the television programs and commercials that he had done, DiCaprio had gained a great deal of experience that led him to his next career role: that of moviestar.

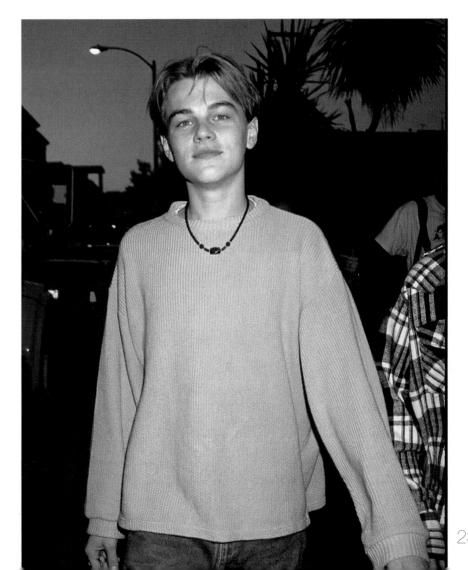

This Boy's Life

In *This Boy's Life*, Leonardo landed his first serious acting role.

W hile he was still in the middle of filming television commercials, work in two different feature films came up. The first one was the shlocky horror flick *Critters 3* (1991), and the second one was the titillating sex and suspense hit *Poison Ivy* (1992).

To this day, Leonardo hates to admit that he had anything to do with either of these movies, but the fact of the matter is that they were important stepping stones in his career. In *Critters 3* Leo played one of the teenagers terrorized by a bunch of furballs from outer space. The special effects are so low-tech that upon first sight, these menacing creatures look more like something a cat coughed up than creatures to fear. This is a film that Leonardo—to this day—refuses to talk about, like an embarrassment from his past. It is admittedly nothing short of dreadful. Cheesy special effects, a lame plot, and bad dialogue mar the campy horror movie potential the material could have lent itself to becoming. Instead, the creatures look like killer Muppets from outer space and the human actors do their best to elevate the proceedings. Neither Leonardo DiCaprio nor seasoned character actress Diana Bellamy could save this truly bad B movie.

His next film appearance was in the decidedly better *Poison Ivy*. Unfortunately, Leo's part in it is nothing more than a glorified extra role. In *Poison Ivy*, you have to look very closely to even find Leonardo in his fleeting scene at the beginning of the film. His brief role as Guy is little more than a billed extra role in

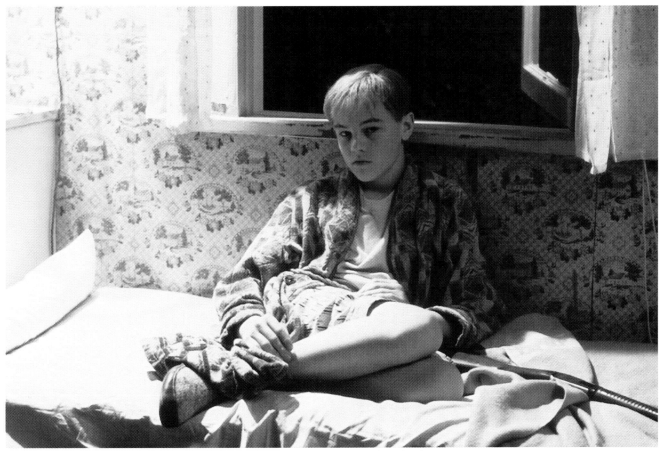

Leonardo brought to the screen the role of Toby in Tobias Wolff's beloved coming-of-age book.

It was in *Critters 3* that DiCaprio made his movie debut.

this Drew Barrymore / Sara Gilbert vehicle about a *Bad Seed* kind of teenager infiltrating a family—with deadly results. Locating him on screen is kind of like looking for the cartoon character Waldo in one of those *Where's Waldo?* books. A film classic compared to *Critters 3, Poison Ivy* is a creepy, sexy sizzler that is totally entertaining. In the context of the film, Drew is invited to move in with an upper class household because of her offbeat charms. Along the way she charms Cheryl Ladd, who plays a self-suffering hypochondriac. Then she physically seduces both Sara Gilbert and Tom Skerritt. If you're quick you can spot Leonardo in a group scene at the beginning of the film, for only a few brief moments.

While these first two films are totally disregarded by DiCaprio, they bear witness to a budding career in the making. Although neither movie posed any dramatic challenges for Leonardo, they were crucial in giving him his first legitimate cinematic experiences. With these two films under his belt, it was now time for a real meaty role in which he could show off his true acting talent. And what a great role he ended up with!

Explaining his career evolution to this point, Leo recalls, "I did about thirty, forty commercials, then I got *Growing Pains* during eleventh grade and for twelfth grade I had home study. I did twenty-four episodes and toward the end of that I auditioned for *This Boy's Life.*"

Going through the audition for *This Boy's Life* was an adventure unto itself. First and foremost was the fact that he had to audition with none other than Robert DeNiro himself. Between doing his first two films, *Growing Pains* and *Parenthood*, television commercials, and his schoolwork, Leonardo didn't have a lot of time to indulge in any starstruck idol worship. While most teenagers his age might have been dumbfounded at the prospect of actually auditioning with someone of the stature of Robert DeNiro, Leo just viewed it as an audition with another actor . . . period. He didn't stop to think about DeNiro's stature in the business when he arrived for the tryout for the role of Toby in this screen adaptation of Tobias Wolff's autobiographical book.

According to DiCaprio, "'My ignorance,' as Toby says, 'was a kind of advantage.' Anyway, I stood up in front of DeNiro really forcefully and I pointed at his face and screamed one of the lines. Then I sat there and waited for some kind of reaction. I remember DeNiro had this smirk on his face, like, obviously [he knew] this kid wanted to come in here and show him that he had guts. Everyone started laughing and I said, 'What? What is it?' And, well, the cool thing is that I obviously showed him something."

Looking back in retrospect, Leo explains, "I got the part by just going in and doing it, no mumbo jumbo. I didn't worry what DeNiro thought. I went in, looked him in the eye and got the part. I was confident, even though I'd never done anything like it before. Now I realize it was ignorant confidence. I had no idea!"

The film opens with Leonardo DiCaprio and Ellen Barkin driving across the beautiful countryside of the American Southwest. They portray Toby and Carolyn, a mother and son on the run. In Leo's narrative voice we learn that his mother has broken off with her latest physically abusive boyfriend, and they are running away from Florida, on their way to Utah. When things go "bust" in Utah, they jump in a bus and head for the Pacific Northwest. Things really shift dramatically with the introduction of Dwight (Robert

"I didn't worry what DeNiro thought. I went in, looked him in the eye and got the part. I was confident, even though I'd never done anything like it before."

Ellen Barkin, Leonardo DiCaprio, and Robert DeNiro in *This Boy's Life*.

DeNiro)—the man destined to become Toby's stepfather-from-Hell.

At the beginning, the film seems as if it is going to unfold like a parent and child *Thelma and Louise*. However, it soon hits high gear to become an emotional tour de force for DiCaprio, DeNiro, and Barkin. A conservative tough guy with a mean streak, Dwight is an obsessive-compulsive personality with the compassion of a dictator. When young Toby gets into a bad crowd of hoodlum kids, Dwight is enlisted by Carolyn as the surrogate father figure she feels her son needs. Instead of just disciplining Toby, and keeping him from wasting his life hanging out with a bunch of losers, Dwight soon turns into a physically abusive bully of a parent.

This Boy's Life is a first-rate film that is very emotionally charged, beautifully filmed, and totally enter-taining. Besides which, Leonardo DiCaprio is incredibly impressive as Toby, a boy struggling to find himself. This was the beginning of Leo's career typecasting as a troubled youth on the big screen. In this coming-of-age film set in the late 1950s and early 1960s, DiCaprio brilliantly holds his own in the company of DeNiro and Barkin, two of the biggest stars of 1990s American cinema.

Speaking of the role of Toby and his interaction with DeNiro's character, Leo admits, "Toby was a little snot who needed someone strict. But he didn't need a maniac like his stepfather, Dwight. Dwight took strictness to another level." Indeed, in the context of the film, a little bit of disciplinary action goes a long way!

Being in puberty at the time, during the ten weeks of filming *This Boy's Life*, Leonardo reportedly grew a full four inches taller. In several of the scenes that they shot, Leonardo had to crouch down so he didn't appear taller than Robert DeNiro! With regard to the physically demanding scenes in the movie, Leo recalls receiving a few black and blue marks from the shoot. There is one particular scene in the film where DeNiro gives DiCaprio fistfighting lessons, and things get a little out of hand. "I got a couple of bruises from big old Bobby D," Leonardo laughs.

Unlike the teenage films such as *Critters 3* and *Poison Ivy*, *This Boy's Life* represented a really major career move for Leo. After he was finished filming it, DiCaprio had nothing but glowing things to say about the man who starred in the film.

"Robert DeNiro is one of the greatest actors who ever lived. That just suddenly hit me when I realized I had the part in *This Boy's Life*. I learned a lot from his professionalism, from his focus. But I don't work the same way he does. It would take a lot of work for me to get into the role that much. He gets totally, but totally, involved in the character. Me? I come in, do the work and walk away so that I can be myself."

The stakes were beginning to heat up for this blond young actor. After viewing his acting in *This Boy's Life*, David Ansen in *Newsweek* magazine referred to him as "the astonishingly talented Leonardo DiCaprio."

Although Leo was thrilled with what his career was presently doing, he was already projecting himself into the future. "I got to turn into a man," he says of his part in this coming-of-age story. "There are a lot more roles for young men than old teenagers." Little did he know, but there were still some prime "old teenager" roles to come for him, and some damn good ones at that!

Leo was able to show many sides of his personality in *This Boy's Life*.

Leo at the premiere of *What's Eating Gilbert Grape?* on the Paramount Studios lot.

What's Eating Leo DiCaprio?

T o have been seen in such a prestigious film as *This Boy's Life*, Leonardo's acting career was really starting to get some acclaim in the film world. Now that he was finished with high school, it was also time for him to decide what he wanted to do about his studies. During this era, when he was asked if he would be continuing his education, he simply replied, "Life is my college for now."

Choosing his next project was to prove a bit of a dilemma for Leonardo. "I didn't know where I was gonna go as an actor so I didn't know what types of movies I wanted to do," he explains. "I just felt like doing a movie is doing a movie. I get money and fame, and that's great, and I can act and have fun. And I was up for a movie called *Hocus Pocus,* with Bette Midler, and I knew it was awful, but it was just like, 'Okay, they're offering me more and more money. Isn't that what you do? You do movies and you get more and more money.' But something inside of me kept saying,

After *Gilbert Grape* came along, Leonardo found himself sitting in a very exciting spot.

31

As his career heated up, DiCaprio had a lot to smile about

Grape. If I don't get that, I'll do *Hocus Pocus.* I found myself trying so hard, investing so much time and energy in *Gilbert Grape,* I worked so damn hard at it and I finally got it, and it was like such a weight off my shoulders."

It was actually quite a fortunate turn of events for Leo. *Hocus Pocus* turned out to be quite a bomb at the box office, despite the fact that it starred red hot Bette Midler. *What's Eating Gilbert Grape?* ultimately gave him the opportunity to really stretch out acting-wise, and to truly immerse himself in the character of Arnie Grape. SinceArnie was mentally retarded, this really was going to be a true challenge for him. The cast also included two of the hottest young actors in Hollywood: Johnny Depp and Juliette Lewis.

Leonardo claims that he relied a lot on instinct while bringing the role of Arnie to life on screen. "When I did *What's Eating Gilbert Grape?* I had no particular pressure on me," he says. "Now I feel there is more pressure on me to keep to that same text that I've kept to in my past two movies, or just maintaining my natural ability. I didn't even know what I did in *Gilbert Grape.* I just went off with whatever I felt instinc-

'Don't do this movie.' And everyone around me was saying, 'Leonardo, how could you not take a movie?' And I said to myself, 'Okay, I'll audition for this movie *Gilbert*

tually without a second thought."

In the role of mentally handicapped Arnie Grape, Leonardo DiCaprio turns in one of the most riveting portrayals of his career. Set in the midwestern town of Eudora, *What's Eating Gilbert Grape?* centers on the life of Arnie and his siblings. The screenplay is one of quirky fascination, filmed in a town that is both gray and dismal. Starring heartthrob Johnny Depp as the pressured older brother in the Grape household, the entire family is ridiculed and made fun of by their neighbors and the local townspeople.

The children's father has long been missing from the household, as he committed suicide several years ago. Since the time of the suicide, their mother (Darlene Cates), has never left the house, let alone the living room sofa of the wooden farmhouse in which she and her children dwell. Since her husband's tragic death, she has insulated herself from reality by eating, and eating, and eating, until she has reached her present weight, in the 400-pound vicinity.

The mental weight of maintaining some sort of social dignity, and some sort of normal household existence, has fallen on the shoulders

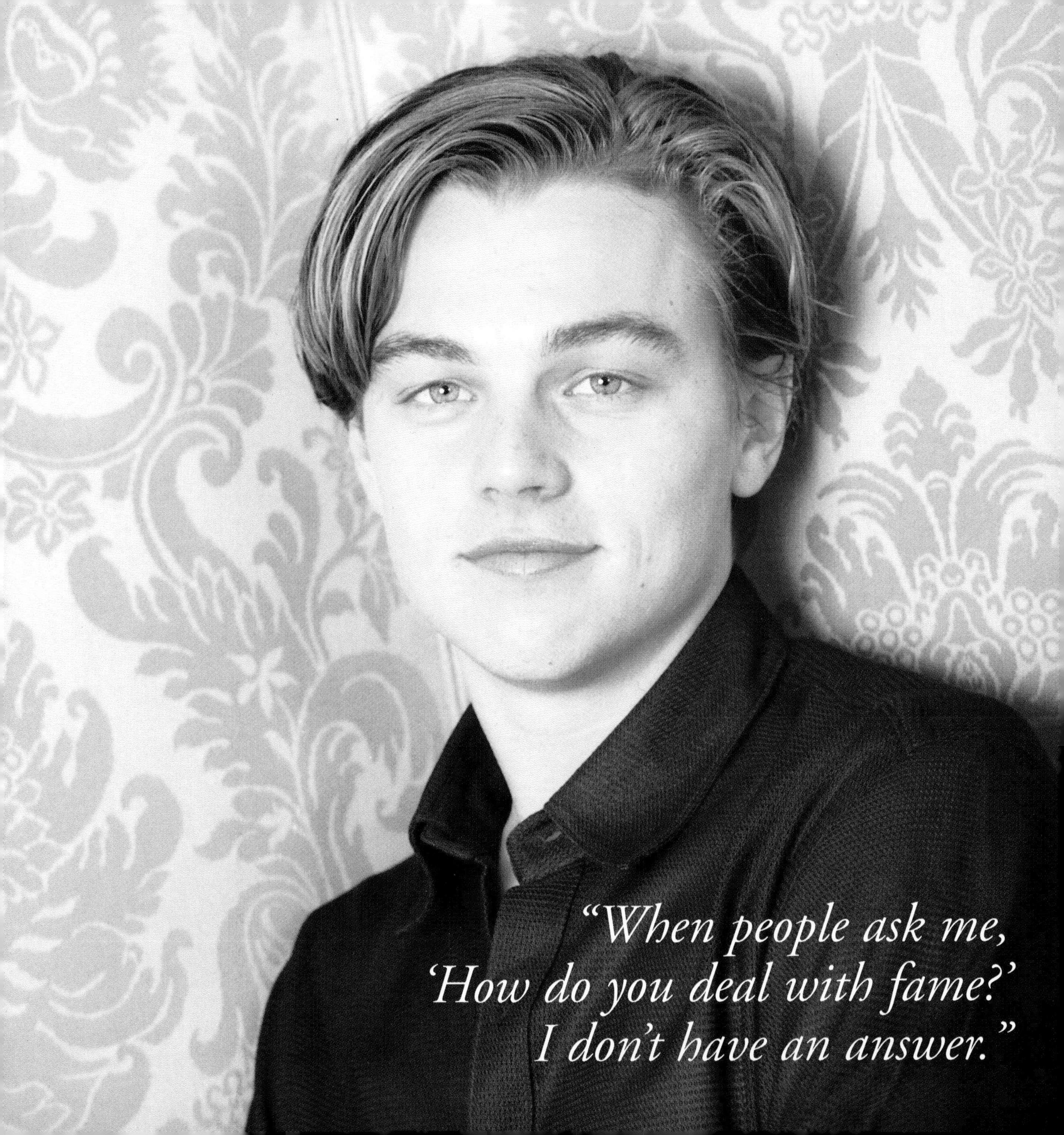

"When people ask me,
'How do you deal with fame?'
I don't have an answer."

of Gilbert (Johnny Depp) and his sisters Amy (Laura Harrington) and Ellen (Mary Kate Schellhardt). In an effort to hold on to his sanity, Gilbert has been carrying on a sexual affair with a local homemaker (Mary Steenburgen), and holding steadfastly to a dead-end job at the local family-owned Lanson's grocery store.

Gilbert has a lot of emotional problems eating at him. He has to chase cruel name-calling local children from the family's window sills as they point to and laugh at his enormous mother. He has to earn money to support the family. He has to keep his affair with Mrs. Carver a secret, care for his mother and his siblings, and he consistently has to try to keep Arnie from getting into trouble. All of his emotions are further magnified when a young girl named Beckie (Juliette Lewis) rolls into town with her grandmother.

Leonardo's portrayal of Arnie is touching, focused, and effused with a sense of innocence and frustration. He clearly has connected with the spirit of the character, and kept Arnie from becoming a comic sight gag or a one-dimensional cripple. A

The cast of *What's Eating Gilbert Grape?* (clockwise from the top) Johnny Depp, Juliette Lewis, Darlene Cates, Mary Kate Schellhardt, Leonardo DiCaprio, and Laura Harrington.

childlike wonderment seems to emanate from his eyes as he grapples to understand ideas and situations far beyond his grasp.

Much to Gilbert's horror, one of Arnie's favorite activities is climbing up the ladder of Eudora's massive steel water tower. Whenever anyone is preoccupied with other business and he has a clear shot at the first step on the ladder, up climbs Arnie, hundreds of feet in the air. This dangerous hobby is also performed much to the chagrin of the local fire department, which is constantly called in to pluck him from his galvanized steel perch on the water tower. When Arnie is finally arrested for climbing up this gigantic municipal structure, the Grape family is thrown into turmoil.

In spite of the ridicule that the children's huge mother is sure to face by going out in public for the first time in years, she braves it, and defiantly marches to the local police station to set things straight. At the cathartic conclusion of the film, the Grape children are faced with a dramatic decision when their mother perishes.

A truly odd and offbeat film about love and family ties, *What's Eating Gilbert Grape?* transcended its expectations as a cult film to find mainstream acceptance and it became a major box office hit. Leonardo won attention and critical acclaim for his portrayal of Arnie, and turned in the most pivotal and important acting job of his four-film silver screen career.

Actors very often zero-in on some aspect of their own personality to bring a fictional character to life. Were there any traits in Arnie that Leo found to be similar? "Just in a couple of ways," he says, "but I would really like to be as sponta-

"I didn't even know what I did in Gilbert Grape. I just went off with whatever I felt instinctually without a second thought."

Leo, under arrest, as Arnie Grape.

Leonardo, with Johnny Depp and Juliette Lewis, brought a poignant performance to *What's Eating Gilbert Grape?*

Arnie dissolved into tears when he realized he had beheaded his grasshopper.

neous and carefree as him. He is very instinctive; just speaks off the top of his head. He is not able to comprehend that a statement might hurt someone or that it's inappropriate to say for other reasons—he just says it because he's got no sense of judgment and no inhibitions. Arnie is very needy, and I am definitely not like that. He always has to be watched like a four-year-old or he may accidentally kill himself. He has no sense of right or wrong, because he's mentally retarded—it's not because he wasn't raised right."

There is one particular scene in which Arnie beheads a grasshopper guillotine-style, using a mailbox closure. He is then horrified that he has inadvertently killed his pet insect. "Animal rights activists are going to have MY head for this one!" he laughed at the time, explaining, "I was supposed to do a scene where Arnie slams the head off a grasshopper in the family mailbox. There were actually animal rights activists on the set to ensure that we really didn't do it, but I didn't know this. So I put the grasshopper in the mailbox and the director decides to shoot the rehearsal and I just smashed the poor thing's head off. I think the director was hoping I'd do

that because he thought it was ridiculous that these activists had to be there to monitor things. He was a little annoyed."

DiCaprio turned in a wonderful performance, winning the approval and praise of his coworkers and critics alike.

Speaking of Leonardo's ability to lose himself in the role of Arnie, director Lasse Hallström theorizes, "It comes very easy to him. My only theory is that he has a connection to the four-year-old inside." Hallström also predicted at the time, "I am

convinced he is, as you say in America, 'star material.'"

Not only was he impressed, but so were his acting peers. In February of 1994, the name of Leonardo DiCaprio was included in the Academy Award nominations in the category of Best Supporting Actor for his portrayal of Arnie in *What's Eating Gilbert Grape?* The other nominees included Ralph Fiennes for *Schindler's List*, Tommy Lee Jones for *The Fugitive*, John Malkovich for *In the Line of Fire*, and Pete Postlethwaite for *In the*

Leonardo and his Gilbert Grape mother, Darlene Cates, at the film's premiere.

Name of the Father.

This was not only a huge honor, but it really signaled a major acting career in the making. Although Leo was excited and honored himself, he was also terrified of actually winning an Oscar, and having to stand up and deliver an acceptance speech. "The Academy Awards was a big burden for me, because of my problem of speaking in front of big audiences," he claims. "I'm doing a lot better with it now, but it was just this gut-wrenching fear of slipping up and doing something horrible . . . or crying, or doing something that's embarrassing, because I'm so critical of other people. When I watch people who do that, I go, 'Oh God, what a f***in' idiot.' And I put that pressure on myself. So I was dreading winning. It was like this weight on my shoulders for so long and there were some people who were saying, 'Hey, you might have a chance.' And I was saying, 'No, no, I'm not gonna win.' And I was convincing myself and I said, 'I'm not ever gonna plan a speech because I know I'm not gonna win.'"

When the big night arrived, Leonardo was a nervous wreck, because he knew in his heart that he truly DID have a shot at winning the award. Proud of what he had accomplished, he invited his mother, his father, and Peggy to be with him. He recalls, "I was so nervous, and when I get nervous, my palms start to sweat, and I just start to twitch, sort of like an animal. And then I came to the awards and people started telling me, 'You know what, you have a pretty good chance of winning tonight.' And this thing started to consume me and I started shaking in my seat

Leonardo and his mother at the 1994 Golden Globe Awards.

and having this posed smile, and inside being petrified. And mine was the first one up, and my mom had to go to the bathroom. And they said, 'Okay, the nominees for Best Supporting Actor . . .' and my mom wasn't there! And I knew if my mom wasn't there, it would be terrible. I saw the guard holding my mom back. She was trying to jump through a bunch of people, and they showed the first person, and said, 'Tommy Lee Jones in *The Fugitive*.' I knew I had to do something: my mom HAD TO BE next to me. So I turned to the security guards and I mouthed, 'Let her f***ing in!' And then the guy looked at me, and I said, 'I'm a nominee.' I never do that kind of shit, but I figured this was really important."

Leonardo was able to whisk his mother back through the security guards and into her seat just in time for the winner to be announced. According to Leonardo, "Mean-while, I'm about ready to die. And

Leonardo and his mother at the *Gilbert Grape* premiere.

when they announced Tommy Lee Jones had won, I wanted to get down on the ground and thank God. Nobody was happier for him than me, that's the f***ing truth!"

Whether he intended it to happen or not, Leonardo DiCaprio was becoming a huge star. "I know I've changed," he admits. "No matter what, becoming well known makes your mind start thinking in a different way. For example, people are watching you a lot more than they ever were. When people ask me, 'How do you deal with fame?' I don't have an answer. When a person comes to me and says, 'I really enjoyed your performance,' I try to give a sincere 'thank you,' but I have no way to show you that I'm a decent guy and that I respect what you're saying."

It is easy to act in a movie on a closed set and go on about your life without considering what the consequences will be—good or bad. Well, like it or not, he had to get used to this new phenomenon of fame. Due to *What's Eating Gilbert Grape?* and the Academy Awards nomination, everyone suddenly seemed to know the name Leonardo DiCaprio.

(clockwise, from above left)

Leonardo with model Kristen Zang. They dated for fifteen months.

With actress Gwyneth Paltrow.

Leo and his grandmother at the Cannes Film Festival.

Romeo and his Juliet, Claire Danes.

DiCaprio with Gillian Anderson of TV's *X Files*.

Leonardo Scores

When it finally came time to cast *The Basketball Diaries*, it was lucky DiCaprio who landed the role.

In 1993, one of the most hotly discussed upcoming films in Hollywood was the film version of Anne Rice's *Interview with the Vampire*. It seemed like every young leading man in Hollywood was under consideration for one role or another. As prized as the roles of the main vampires—Louis and Lestat—were, there was also the role of the interviewer to cast. In preproduction, it was Leo's idol River Phoenix who had landed that plum role.

Although Leo and River ran around in social circles that intersected, they were never formally introduced.

As the Kid in *The Quick and the Dead*.

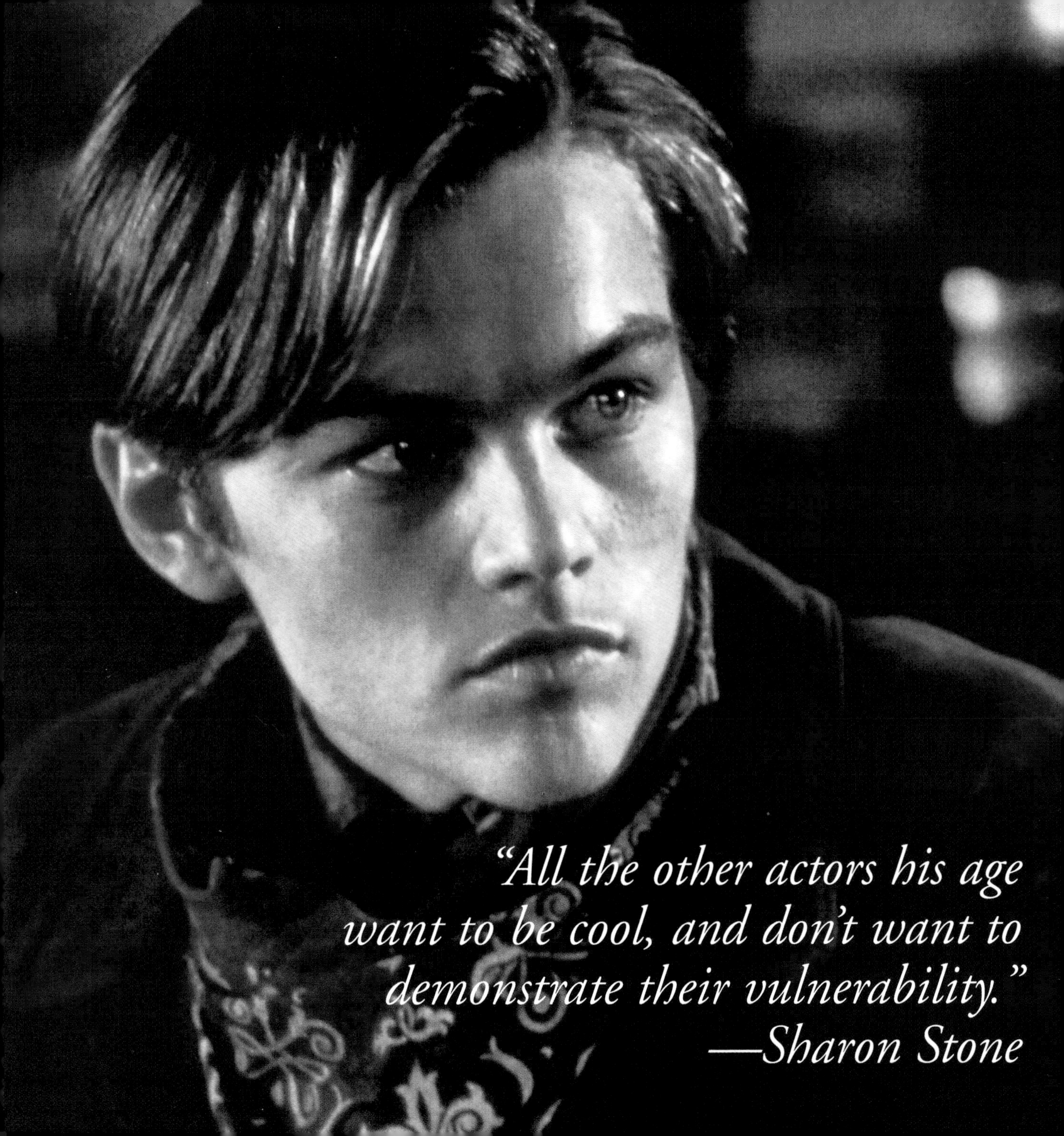

"All the other actors his age want to be cool, and don't want to demonstrate their vulnerability."
—Sharon Stone

Leo as writer Jim Carroll in *The Basketball Diaries*.

Of his only encounter with River, recalls DiCaprio, "I was at a Halloween party two years ago [1993] and I remember it was really dark and everyone was drunk and I was passing through these crowds of people so thick it was almost two lanes of traffic, when I glanced at a guy in a mask and suddenly knew it was River Phoenix. I wanted to reach out and say 'hello' because he was this great mystery and we'd never met, and I thought he probably wouldn't blow me off because I'd done stuff by then that was maybe worth watching. But then I got caught in a lane of traffic and slid right past him. The next thing I knew, River had died. That same night."

River accidentally overdosed on drugs at Johnny Depp's infamous Viper Club in Los Angeles, and the role of the interviewer was suddenly left vacant. Almost immediately, DiCaprio's name was among those mentioned for the part. However, he lost out to Christian Slater. It seemed that the casting people thought that Leo still looked a bit too young for the part. Leo claims that he was very disappointed about it at the time.

While all of this was going on,

another prestigious film was finally about to begin production after years of anticipation. It was the screen adaptation of Jim Carroll's *The Basketball Diaries*. Carroll had a hard life when he grew up in New York City in the 1960s, a life that was magnified by his downfall into heroin addiction. The book of poems and essays that he wrote while in his downwardly mobile tailspin had become a cult worshiped book. Rumors of a screen adaptation had been circulating for years. Finally, Island Pictures ended up with the rights to it, and the search for a young star began.

According to Liz Heller, an independent producer for Island Pictures, somehow everything seemed to point to Leonardo starring in *The Basketball Diaries*. "Eight or nine people all in the same day kept saying, 'You should see *This Boy's Life*, that kid would be great as Jim Carroll.'"

When Leonardo was officially slated to star in the film, his Academy Award nomination came along, and suddenly the stakes were dramatically magnified. "The whole dynamic changed," Heller claims.

"*The Basketball Diaries* was the first time where I actually read a

Mark Wahlberg and Leonardo DiCaprio as two teenagers living on the edge.

script and I didn't want to put it down," Leonardo recalls. "Then I met Scott Kalvert, the director, who hadn't done a movie before. He had done these Marky Mark videos. So that was a bit of a problem. I wanted to do this movie, but I didn't want it to turn out to be some *After School Special* about drugs, which is what it could have turned out to be.

But when I met Scott, he seemed like a cool guy. He didn't have all the Hollywood director s*** going on. He was willing to listen to my opinions."

One of the things he was most impressed with on this trip was the contrast between sprawling Los Angeles and compact and intense New York City. "I came to New

York and hung out. It is very different. In California, they'll tell you how great you are. Everyone flatters everyone. In New York, they put you down. They'll tell you the truth. It's good!" he exclaims.

Leonardo soon found himself in The Big Apple on an eight week shooting schedule. Budgeted at $4 million, the film was considered low budget by today's standards. The experience provided Leonardo with several adventures with his costars.

The grimy haunts that *The Basketball Diaries* is played against were among the seediest in all of New York City. Filthy abandoned buildings and dark alleys provided the backdrops for the action. Director Scott Kalvert recalls, "Shooting in New York, it's chaos and pandemonium. The kids were down here in the slime. They worked hard and got grubby. They became real."

Leo's eyes were really opened up by the sights he saw in Manhattan. "Everyone was harping on how much L.A. was blasted," he says. "I was like, 'No man, I love L.A.!' But after I came here, I was like, 'Now I see what you're saying.' I love it! I want to move here. You could sit at one

The Basketball Diaries proved that Leonardo could carry an entire movie, as its star.

corner all day and probably have a more fulfilling day than traveling all over L.A. and seeing all the sights."

The Basketball Diaries was the first feature film that starred Leonardo DiCaprio above the title, and showed him off as a captivating actor with the ability to carry the weight of an entire film. When all was said and done, he passed the test with flying colors! Ever since *This Boy's Life*, he has portrayed one troubled young man after another, and portraying Jim Carroll really allowed him to crystallize his ability to portray neurotic dysfunctionality to a tee.

In one of the first scenes of the film, we see Leo as Carroll, together with his school buddies, sniffing cleaning fluid on the Staten Island ferry as an after school pastime. This scene perfectly sets the prevailing tone for the whole movie: drugs, drugs, and more drugs. Drugs for kicks, drugs for escape, and finally—drugs merely for survival.

To portray this role with stunning realism, Leonardo really had to mine the depths of his soul to show scenes of cruelty, humiliation, drug withdrawal, prostitution, and finally redemption.

As skinny and wiry Jim Carroll,

Leonardo not only had to bring a sense of believability to the drug scenes, but he also had to learn to become a proficient basketball player as well. In a very short time, he slips downward in a spiral from being one of his school team's star players into a full-fledged junkie. Along the way, he has to face the leukemia death of one of his team-

mates, de? with the sexual advances of his basketball coach, and before he hits bottom, he finds himself facing a life-and-death existence on the streets of New York when his mother throws him out of the house.

His costars included the charismatic Mark Wahlberg [the former Marky Mark], Bruno Kirby, Ernie

Mark Wahlberg, director Scott Kalvert, James Madio, Patrick McGaw, and Leo, amidst the filming *The Basketball Diaries*.

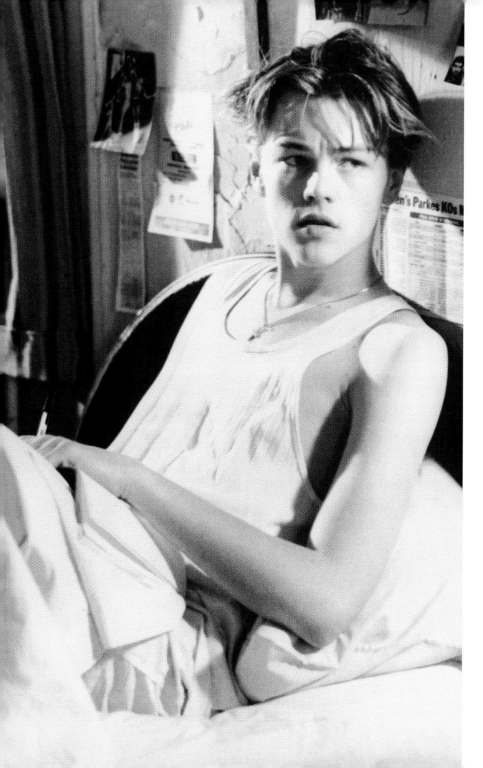

Hudson, Marilyn Sokol, and Lorraine Bracco—as his long suffering mother. Throughout the film, Leonardo is absolutely captivating as he runs the emotional gamut from elation to desperation, and back again. In the final scenes, we see the recovery of Jim Carroll, celebrating his life after his last "dry out," reading poetry in a Greenwich Village coffeehouse. A grimy, frank, and depressing film, *The Basketball Diaries* brilliantly proved that Leonardo DiCaprio could throw himself into a role, carry an entire film, and emerge a dedicated and likable actor, in spite of the film's subject matter.

"It's certainly not a film that glorifies drugs," explains Leo. "It doesn't preach things like 'Just say no' either. What it shows is that the first hit can be the start of real trouble. This movie took me places I'd never been before, acting wise. Withdrawal was the hardest thing to play. It's like being an animal, in a primal state."

A film as stark and grimy as its subject matter, *The Basketball Diaries* not only cemented Leo's Hollywood

Amidst his descent into drug addiction, it was Jim Carroll's personal diaries that kept him sane. Leo was powerful as self-destructive Carroll.

Patrick McGaw as Neutron, James Madio as Pedro, Mark Wahlberg as Mickey, and Leonardo DiCaprio as Jim.

"bad boy" image on camera, but off camera as well. As DiCaprio, Marky Mark, and the rest of the young cast members hit the streets to party in New York City, the gossip columnists had a field day getting their first glimpse at this hot new Academy Award–nominated actor. By the time they were finished, they had branded him a "party animal" of the most irresponsible kind.

"He seldom sleeps, so intense is his partying. Juliette Lewis and Leonardo DiCaprio—two lovebirds who seldom rest in the nest—were all over each other at Rouge the other night . . . " reported top gossip columnist Liz Smith. "He hits Manhattan clubs . . . and brawls with the locals . . . " claimed *The New York Post*. And *Rolling Stone* magazine scolded, "He seems poised to assume the mantle of River Phoenix . . . "

At first he was very startled at the way the press followed his every move. "They want to title me the 'Young Hollywood Hotshot Who All of a Sudden Goes Rampant.' They don't see me hanging out in my hotel room or doing whatever normal things I do," he complained.

Now that he was famous, he found that he couldn't do things in an incognito fashion anymore. "I'm a 20-year-old guy who goes out with my friends," he said in effort to explain his sudden not-so-favorable notoriety. "My mistake is that I think I can actually be like a normal human being and have fun and go to normal places. I'm realizing that I have to lead a sheltered life, where I watch out for everything I do. I certainly don't think I'm leading a destructive lifestyle, at least compared to other people my age. I just try to loosen up after work."

In his own eyes, he worked hard on his films, and when he wanted to let loose, he definitely threw himself into that as well. "I mean, I haven't gone crazy yet, and I really do think I'm pretty well-balanced being in the position I'm in. I think it has to do with me not investing everything in my job. All these actors think that the blood through their veins is fueled by acting. I'm happier when I'm not working, hanging out with my friends, doing something I love," he says, explaining his penchant for pleasure.

Leonardo admits that working on *The Basketball Diaries* certainly did lend itself to partying heavily with his costars. "They make it sound like I go to clubs and wreck myself silly, get into fights, sleep with all the ratty girls there. It's true that while we were filming, Marky and I went out for a little dancing, a little socializing, a little flirting. And one morning we wake up to find that, according to the paper, I picked a fight with Derrick Coleman, forward for the New Jersey Nets! Like I'm going to get into an argument with him. Yo, Derrick! He's six-foot-a-hundred! He could spill a drink on me, and I'm not going to fight."

Madio, Wahlberg, McGaw, and DiCaprio in New York City.

"I came to New York and hung out. It is very different. In California, they'll tell you how great you are. Everyone flatters every-one. In New York, they put you down. They'll tell you the truth. It's good!" he exclaims.

Leonardo and Gene Hackman as son and father in conflict in *The Quick and the Dead*.

At the time, he was romantically linked with his costars Sara Gilbert and Juliette Lewis. . . . He says, "They're just my friends. Can't I have friends? . . . But people want you to be a crazy, out-of-control teen brat. They want you miserable, just like them. They don't want heroes; what they want is to see you fall."

However, Leonardo does admit that there was some truth to the rumors. "I sort of got into a fight in L.A. a couple of months ago," he admitted in 1994. "I drank a little—tequila as a matter of fact—and I sort of took on a different personality and kind of picked on a kid on purpose, and really pushed him to the edge. I was playing a role, a tough-guy thing. I really was looking for a fight, and I sort of hurt the kid a little bit. It was a mistake, and I felt so guilty afterwards."

His bad boy image certainly didn't hurt the publicity for *The Basketball Diaries* when it was released. It became something of a cult hit, and Leonardo received further glowing reviews for his acting. He was suddenly a hot property in Hollywood. After he was finished working on *The Basketball Diaries*, Sharon Stone was looking for a young actor to portray the role of the Kid in a forthcoming departure film for her: the offbeat western, *The Quick and the Dead*. After her recent film success in several sexy femme fatale roles, she was looking for something different. With *The Quick and the Dead*, she found just such a role. Poised to portray a tough-as-nails lady gunslinger in the Wild West of the late nineteenth century, Stone wanted to be surrounded by a stellar supporting cast of characters.

Stone claimed that she really wanted Leonardo very badly: "All the other actors his age want to be cool, and don't want to demonstrate their vulnerability."

Leonardo recalls that agreeing to appear in a western was not necessarily his first choice. "With *The Quick and the Dead*, I really had to think it through for a long time. It was honestly not my idea of the type of movie that I wanted to do next. I turned it down like at least 10 to 20 times. Then on the last day they said, 'Hey look, they really want you, and this is the last day you can have the role, because they're gonna hire somebody else.' Everyone around me was saying, 'Look, this is a good movie.' I had this thing about not doing big commercial movies because all the big commercial movies, not all of them, but most of the mainstream movies are just pieces of garbage that have been done over thousands of times. But

DiCaprio with Gene Hackman, Sharon Stone, and Russell Crow as gunslingers in *The Quick and the Dead.*

Quick-draw DiCaprio: the Kid, involved in a deadly game of gunplay.

then I looked at *The Quick and the Dead*, and I thought, 'Okay, Sharon Stone's in it,' and I think—disregarding her superstardom—'the woman definitely has something going on, and Gene Hackman's in it, and Sam Raimi is a completely innovative director. My character's somebody that's so completely insecure in himself that he has to put on a show to dazzle everybody,' and that to me started some interest."

The Quick and the Dead is a stylized, bizarre, and unlikely western, which makes fun of the film genre in the same tongue-in-cheek style as Clint Eastwood's *The Good, the Bad, and the Ugly*. In the plot of the film, Darryl Cooper (Sharon Stone) rides into a dusty Arizona Territory town just in time for a fiesta, and a gunfighting contest with a huge cash prize. Whether by will or by threat, all of the fastest gunslingers in town sign up for this deadly competition, for cash and potential control of the town. Part of the ground rules are that an entrant cannot refuse the challenge of another contestant.

Included in the competition to the death are Harod (Gene Hackman), who has monetary control of the town, and his teenage son, the Kid (Leonardo DiCaprio). The rest of the contest is peopled with a scurvy looking batch of desperate characters. To add some genuine western movie flavor, veteran actors like Pat Hingle are mixed in with newer stars like Russell Crowe, Woody Strode, and Gary Sinise.

Leonardo plays the Kid with cocky bravado. In his first challenge, the Kid wins his duel against a fat, bearded, bald desperado, and is carried through the streets on everyone's shoulders like a conquering hero. For his second challenge, he is convinced that he can win in this one-on-one gun battle against the one man he despises the most—yet wants to impress the most: his own father. Unfortunately, his gamble has disastrous consequences.

Even as the warrior heroine of the film, Darryl has mixed results as a gunslinger. She is easily able to kill her first scuzzy opponent, much to the town's surprise. Her second battle ends with her bleeding in the streets. Stark reality, however, has nothing to do with the plot of this film, so when she appears to resurrect herself from the dead to blow up the whole town in a dramatic act of vengeance, it somehow fits the loopy logic of the rest of the film.

At the age of nineteen, Leonardo DiCaprio holds his own in this town of unsavory characters, looking every inch the fresh-faced young boy he is in real life. Although *The Quick and the Dead* didn't become the major cult hit that it might have blossomed into, it is totally entertaining, as a great off-the-wall showcase for Sharon Stone, and for Leonardo DiCaprio. When it was released in 1995, it received mixed reviews from the critics. *The*

Leo in *Critters 3* (1991)

Chicago Tribune aptly proclaimed, "The movie is quick and slick, but it's far from dead!"

He was also starting to make money, and he was beginning to get comfortable with having it and spending it on significant things. In 1994 Leonardo had one of his proudest moments when he was able to buy his father, George, a car as a birthday present. Leo reveals, "I knew he wanted a new car, because he's had beat-up station wagons all his life. I planned a big fiftieth birthday party for him with all his friends. I had a 'Ska' band there and polka music and he was blowing out candles on the cake in front of his whole family when I pulled up and beeped, and he turned around and it was me with a brand-new car. I couldn't picture anything more beautiful, basically, though I wouldn't tell him that. His face just lit up!"

At this point in time, Leonardo was at the height of his career. From film to film he was gaining in stature, and in fame. He had to be careful of the choices he made from here, as they would be crucial for him to maintain the momentum he currently had going. He already had established for himself a growing

Total Eclipse (1995)

reputation as one of the hottest young actors in Hollywood—now, where was he going with it? Whenever there were choices to be made, it seemed that DiCaprio increasingly chose the path that was the most unpredictable and challenging. For his next three cinematic excursions, he couldn't possibly have found films that were more diametrically different, nor more adventurous.

Twentieth Century Romeo

Total Eclipse represented a whole new departure for Leo.

rom the Wild West setting of his last picture, Leonardo found a direct contrast in the nineteenth century period piece *Total Eclipse*. Like *This Boy's Life* and *The Basketball Diaries*, this was his third film in which he brought to the big screen the portrayal of a real life character. This time it was one straight from the history books.

Total Eclipse depicts the unconventional and short life of nineteenth-century French poet Arthur Rimbaud and his mentor and lover, poet Paul Verlaine. At a time in history when men could be imprisoned for homosexual behavior, Rimbaud was a young punk, thumbing his nose at convention. When he linked up with Verlaine, he ignited something that led the duo into their own world of hard living and substance abuse. *Total Eclipse* is a film about the two poets' life together, their love affair, and the sad endings they both met.

One of the key elements in their self-destructive relationship was absinthe, a highly addictive type of

Diane Keaton and Leonardo DiCaprio in *Marvin's Room* in 1996.

DiCaprio and David Thewlis as French poets Rimbaud and Verlaine.

wood grain alcohol made from the wormwood tree. It was a big hit in nineteenth-century France, but it is also known for ruining lives and leading to insane behavior. Introducing absinthe into the relationship between these two men only intensified their desire to cast caution to the wind—in and out of bed.

Leonardo portrays the crude and unmannered Rimbaud with believable charm. He brings the character to life, as a romantic free spirit, with a gift for expressing his honest poetry in an appealing and imaginative fashion. According to literary history, the poetry Rimbaud wrote between the ages of sixteen and nineteen was viewed as being both brilliant and evocative. When he mailed eight of his poems to

respected poet Paul Verlaine, it caused Verlaine (David Thewlis) to send for Rimbaud, so he could come to learn the ways of a professional poet. It was his poetry that first intrigued Verlaine. However, once Verlaine met sweet-faced and uninhibited Rimbaud, they both soon found themselves on the road to ruin. It wasn't long before Verlaine turned his back on his rich eighteen-year-old wife, and centered all of his sexual attention on Rimbaud.

Total Eclipse was filmed in very gray and sepia tones, accenting the stark, often colorless world that the two poets came from. It is both a ponderous and powerful movie, with very explicit sexual situations depicted between the two men. In time, the brawling, drunken relation-

ship comes to the attention of the authorities, and Verlaine is thrown in prison for acts of perversity.

As a movie role, Leonardo seemed to relish portraying a historical character who was perhaps the poetry world's first "punk." In one particular scene, Leo's Rimbaud disapproves of another poet's public reading, and to display his feelings, he leaps up on the table and urinates on the other man's writing. To say that this film is slightly off the wall is putting it lightly. Told in a slow and deliberate *Masterpiece Theater* kind of style, this story comes to life with a fascinating yet disturbing starkness. The art direction is brilliant, with every other scene looking like a Gustave Caillebotte painting come to life.

It was Rimbaud's total unconventionality that first fascinated Leonardo with the project. "To be that courageous!" he exclaimed of the real-life poet. "Rimbaud wasn't blasé about anything. He did things that were unheard of! If I could just scratch the surface of that—I don't mean to compare myself with him. But I identify."

He was able to empathize with the character's sense of adventure the character's sense of adventure and abandonment. "Thinking about Rimbaud," he pondered, "it seems that artists aren't sure if they're truly artists unless some big disaster happens. I pray that won't happen with me. I respect the gift, but acting is not the biggest deal in the world. If 'the gift' means disaster, I won't go there. There's no guarantees, but I won't be ending up like Rimbaud. You mark my words. So if you hear of any incident about me—a fight, a change of clothes, a little extra gel in the hair . . . don't believe it till you talk to me!"

Prior to filming *Total Eclipse*, Leonardo was welcoming the challenge of portraying the physical tenderness between the two men. "I don't have a problem with doing a film about a relationship of love with another man," he said at the time. "That's just acting, you know what I mean? But as far as the kissing stuff, that's really hard for me, I'm not kidding. But I've faced the fact that I'm gonna have to do it, and I'm gonna do it because I supposedly love the guy. But the movie isn't about homosexuality, although I'm sure that's what the press is gonna be all over."

The role that Leonardo played in *Total Eclipse* is perhaps the world's first Bohemian.

After he had finished acting in the film, Leonardo was pleased by his ability to take chances and portray roles that many actors would be afraid of being seen in. He was insistent that he didn't want to see his career travel down the safe or the obvious route. According to him, "You can't decide on roles for that reason. If it's a great part, and this was, you have to go for it. Very little out there gets me excited. Usually, I

Leonardo portrays the crude and unmannered Rimbaud with believable charm. He brings the character to life, as a romantic free spirit...

The love affair between these two men scandalized nineteenth-century France. The offbeat tone of *Total Eclipse* drew Leo to the project.

possibly be more cliché-ridden?' But I won't lie to you: Staging those scenes was an uncomfortable situation to be in. Thankfully, David [Thewlis] was cool and made things go as well as they could. Yeah, it was risky, but there should be more movies like this. It's the most intelligent film I've been in yet."

The reviews were decidedly mixed when *Total Eclipse* was released in 1995. Although it did not become a huge box-office hit at the time, it has gone on to become a hot film to rent on video. A well-crafted cinematic excursion, this role further solidified Leo's reputation for being predictably unpredictable. According to movie critic Bruce Kirkland in the *Toronto Sun* newspaper, *Total Eclipse* was "Hypnotic! DiCaprio and Thewlis fearlessly delve into the dark lives of poets Rimbaud and Verlaine!"

For his next role, Leonardo brought to the screen a character who was perfect for his stature in the movie business, that of literature's most famous lover: Romeo. One of the key elements to starring in the 1996 production of *William*

Shakespeare's Romeo + Juliet was the fact that the production was going to be totally updated and made relevant and exciting to today's movie-going audience.

Crucial to the success of the film was the on-screen chemistry between Leonardo's Romeo and his Juliet. To play the fourteen-year-old heroine, the film's producers found his perfect partner in Claire Danes. She had the innocence and the strong-willed determination to portray a young woman who would go to any lengths for the man she loved. Previously, Claire had been featured in the pilot for a shot-down Dudley Moore TV series, and then found fame when she landed the starring role in the television sitcom *My So-Called Life*. She was also

directed by Jodie Foster in the hysterically comic dysfunctional family Christmas movie, *Home for the Holidays*. She had displayed the right passion for the role of Juliet to come excitingly to life.

According to Leonardo, "Our *Romeo and Juliet* is a little more hard-core and a lot cooler. Because I wouldn't have done it if I'd had to jump around in tights. If you never read *Romeo and Juliet*, it's like this classic story, blah-blah. But if you really study it, you see Romeo was, like, a gigolo who falls for this girl, Juliet, who says, 'Look, if you've got the balls, put 'em on the table.' It's about those things that carry you in a certain direction and you can't stop; like when people run off to Vegas and get married. That's the beauty of it. They both were people who had guts."

In between takes, Leonardo entertained the cast and crew with his imitations of Michael Jackson and his mimicking each actor's command of their Elizabethan Shakespearean line deliveries. According to costar John Leguizamo, "I'd walk in front of the camera, and Leonardo would do my line all screechy, 'Thou or I must go!' So, the next time I'd become really self-conscious . . . He'd smoke a cigarette, do some laps, do Michael Jackson, go on the set, and there it was," he laughs.

On the set, Claire Danes reported that Leo was quite the clown in between takes: "He did cartwheels and hit people over the head with Twizzlers."

Exciting, evocative, and brilliantly jarring is the 1996 film *William Shakespeare's Romeo + Juliet*. Starring Leonardo as the lovestruck Romeo, and Claire Danes as his Juliet, this totally modern telling of the Bard's immortal classic gave this timeless tale an entirely new spin. This was a very important role for Leonardo, as it was the first time that he has played a romantic hero on screen. Although the plot of the story still presents him as a troubled teen, his troubles stem from a family feud and the undeniable passion of love.

Sprawling modern-day Mexico City, where the film was shot, is the prefect backdrop for conflict and passion in any era. While the look is very much twentieth century, the language is still the standard Elizabethan English in which the play was originally written. The first sight the audience is shown is a TV set, and on the screen is a commentator on the evening news, speaking as though it was 1696 and not 1996. Once you adjust your thinking to your eyes seeing modern yet your ears hearing historic, you get to just sit back and bask in the sometimes stark, sometimes lush sights and sounds of this brilliant production. Although mounting such an anachronism-laden film seems like a gamble, the impressive international cast comes through with shining colors—especially the tragically romantic Leonardo DiCaprio as history's most famous heartthrob.

The play, which was originally set in the fair city of Verona, is now in the class structure-torn status town of Verona Beach, as it is emblazoned on the license plates of grand cars driven by the Montagues and the Capulets. The warring families don't chase each other on horseback with swords; now it is helicopter chases, pistols, and squealing sports cars. The first time we see Leonardo on screen he is at the seaside at sunset, bathed in tangerine light, and looking every inch the romantic hero

In real life Verlaine and Rimbaud risked madness as absinthe addicts. Leonardo relishes playing such dark roles on the screen.

"*Our* Romeo and Juliet
*is a little more hard-core
and a lot cooler.*"

he has grown into over the last couple of years. From the moment he appears on the screen Leo is the perfect embodiment of Romeo: a man so impassioned that he is willing to die for love.

Sumptuously filmed, with lingering close-ups and excitement charged interplays, *William Shakespeare's Romeo + Juliet* is a feast for the eyes. It is truly outrageous to hear the words of the world's most famous playwright delivered over a pool match, or in an elevator. The power play between the two warring families is depicted more like a 1990s gang conflict than a familial power struggle. Played for tongue-in-cheek fun, Juliet's mother is a socially conscious matron who pops diet pills with booze. Marcucio comes to a masquerade as a drag queen, the nurse is a chatty yenta, and the priest who distributes potions looks more like a Hawaiian shirt-clad Timothy Leary than a man of the cloth. Other than that, it is just another day in fair Verona Beach.

Loopy, campy, and done more like an MTV video than a celluloid excursion through the classics,

William Shakespeare's Romeo + Juliet is a beautiful and romantic film, updated to appeal to today's audiences. The first time Romeo sees Juliet, it is through a huge and colorful tropical fish aquarium. Their first kiss is in an elevator, and the famed balcony scene ends with the pair plunging into the backyard swimming pool. When it comes time to show the final interplay between the tragic lovers, their dying scene is in a church laden with so many burning candles, one has to wonder what the oxygen supply was in that exotic church crypt.

For Leonardo, this film let him stretch out a bit on screen and portray the misunderstood Romeo with pensive and introspective gazes. His Romeo is a cigarette-smoking, poetry-reciting renegade with a cause. If he wasn't seen in Hollywood as a born romantic lead before this film was released, this clinched the deal. From this point on, Leo's career was solidly based in the big leagues.

Romancin' Romeo! Leonardo as the world's most famous lover, with Claire Danes as his Juliet.

In *William Shakespeare's Romeo + Juliet*, the streets of Mexico City portrayed Verona in this modern day telling of the classic story of ill-fated love.

Leonardo as Romeo on the run!

As the lovestruck Romeo...this was a very important role for Leonardo, as this is the first time he has played a romantic hero on screen.

According to DiCaprio, "Well, it was an interesting character, once I really started to research him. Because you have this preplanned idea of *Romeo and Juliet*, and what Romeo is supposed to be—just some fluffy, romantic type of guy. But then you realize he was a hopeless romantic, and then he meets Juliet. And Juliet says, 'All right, look: if you've got any real balls, you should marry me now, and risk everything.' So he risks everything—his whole, entire, his whole family, everything—and he marries this girl, which is such an honorable thing to do if you really believe in love like that, especially at that age. It's the ultimate love story. It's a masterpiece."

What made it a unique experience for him? "I think the manner in which we spoke, and the way things were sort of made out to be a lot more clear—not having some sort of affected English accent, and my surroundings with the car—made everything a lot more close to home," he says. "I think Shakespeare would have wanted his work to live on through the years and become a timeless piece that could adapt to the future." And "live on" it did. When the film was released, it hit number one on *Variety* magazine's box-office tally. There were also two separate soundtracks from the film: one with just the atmosphere music and one with the rock & roll tracks featured in the film.

Although he has now performed Shakespeare credibly and adeptly, would he consider doing so live on stage? Not likely, he reports: "Stage work frightens me, I have to say. Just doing something in front of a live audience gives me the willies! And

I've never been accustomed to that. But I'll see. I'm gonna try a bunch of different things in the future."

At the end of 1996, Leonardo was seen in his next film, the well-praised and dramatic *Marvin's Room*. He was brought into the prestigious production partially because his friend Robert DeNiro was one of the coproducers. He found himself acting beside such industry heavyweights as Meryl Streep, Diane

Keaton, Gwen Verdon, and Hume Cronyn.

In *Marvin's Room* Leonardo was able to take another brilliant career turn while portraying a troubled teen whose family is in crisis. The plot centers around Bessie (Diane Keaton), who has just been diagnosed as having cancer. The compassionate Dr. Wally (Robert DeNiro) explains to her that her only solid shot at recovery would be

Harold Perrineau as Marcucio to DiCaprio's Romeo.

A wild, loopy production of this classic, Leonardo played the ultimate romantic hero in *William Shakespeare's Romeo + Juliet.*

a bone marrow transplant from someone close to her own genetic makeup. Her closest healthy relatives are her long-estranged sister Lee (Meryl Streep), and Lee's young sons Hank (Leonardo DiCaprio) and Charlie (Hal Scardino).

Meanwhile, for all these years the sisters have lived at opposite ends of an emotional and geographic abyss. Bessie has remained in Florida, caring for her bedridden father, Marvin (Hume Cronyn), and her slightly dotty Aunt Ruth (Gwen Verdon). What unfolds is a touching close-up view of a dysfunctional family in crisis.

As Hank, Leonardo looks great on the screen. His formerly spotty complexion had cleared up, and he was looking less like a pubescent teen and more like a handsome young man. Acting in this ensemble of total professionals, he delivered a solid portrayal and garnered favorable reviews.

In the first scenes of the movie, we see Hank thumbing through a stack of family photos, dousing them in lighter fluid, and setting the house on fire. He is arrested, and the next time we see him, he is in restraints. Meryl is hysterical as his totally inept mother. She clearly has fun portraying sheer "trailer trash," as she binges on junk food and chain smokes her way through the role.

According to Leonardo, he had a great time working with Streep, Keaton, and DeNiro. "Meryl Streep is completely unlike any other actress I've ever worked with," he says, "just because I've never met anybody who could walk onto a set and—without saying anything—have complete and utter respect. I mean, everybody becomes silent when she walks in and it's this thing that she has when she acts . . . When I did my first scene with her, she was sort of all over the place doing things. I was like: 'What is she doing? That seems so unlike anything that I've seen before. How's that going to look on camera?' Although she does some wild things sometimes, everything ends up completely natural and real. It was a big shock for me to work with Meryl Streep because I've never worked with an actress like that."

Several of Leonardo's most

impressive scenes are played with Diane Keaton, as the newly discovered Aunt Bessie who loves him unconditionally, unlike his own mother. A touching drama, brilliantly brought to the screen by an incredibly strong cast, Marvin's Room was DiCaprio's most mainstream film to date.

During this same period of time, Leonardo noticed that he was beginning to get more and more press coverage over his every move.

People wanted to know where he was going, who he was hanging out with, and what his life was like. Although he was linked romantically with female friends like Sara Gilbert and Juliette Lewis, the longest relationship that Leonardo has been involved in was with model Kristen Zang. They were together approximately fifteen months.

While his career was hitting exciting heights, during this same period of time, he continued on his

own quest for self-exploration. On June 19, 1996, Leonardo played the daredevil, and nearly perished because of it. As part of a birthday celebration for his friend Justin Herwick, he and Leo went skydiving. Fortunately, they went tandem jumping, with an instructor accompanying them. Leo and his instructor, Harley Powell, dove out of the plane 12,500 feet above the California desert, and as he was instructed, he pulled his rip cord at

Leonardo and Claire Danes, locked in an embrace to last for eternity.

67

5,000 feet. Much to his terror, his parachute didn't open. Powell had to get to Leo to release his emergency back-up parachute cord. Fortunately that one worked as planned. His brilliant acting career could have been tragically cut short that morning.

"I thought I was going to lose my best friend," Justin Herwick said with horrified relief.

With regard to indulging in further life-threatening sports, Leonardo reports, "I like to do things that scare me. Skydiving is just the sickest thing. I made a little video afterward, where I look into the camera all jittery and go, 'Leonardo, if you're watching this, this is your last time skydiving. It's your first life-and-death experience. I want you to learn something from it.'"

"Meryl Streep is completely unlike any other actress I've ever worked with."

Meryl Streep and Leo, as a dysfunctional mother and son in *Marvin's Room*.

Titanic Facts

Time the *Titanic* hit the iceberg in the Atlantic Ocean: 11:40 P.M., April 14, 1912

Number of people aboard the *Titanic* on her maiden voyage: 2,228

Number who perished: 1,523

Time it took for the *Titanic* to sink after the collision: 2 hours 40 minutes

Length of the film *Titanic*: 3 hours 14 minutes

Length of the *Titanic*: 882 feet 9 inches

Length of the model used in the film: 775 feet

Depth in the sea the wreckage of the *Titanic* rests at: 2.5 miles

Location in the Atlantic Ocean: Latitude 41 degrees North, 49 degrees West

Weeks it took to film *Titanic*: 27

Originally scheduled release date of the film: July 2, 1997

Actual release date: December 19, 1997

Titanic

An Epic Role

Leonardo DiCaprio, frozen in time aboard the *Titanic*, the world's most famous oceanliner.

Now, from a 1998 perspective, it seems that the film *Titanic* just came out of left field to become a likely contender as the most successful movie produced in film history. It has turned into an amazing blockbuster box-office hit, garnering fourteen Academy Award nominations, tying a record set in 1951 by *All About Eve*. It has also become a star-making turn for its two lead stars: Kate Winslet and Leonardo DiCaprio.

However, epic films don't just happen overnight. *Titanic* was a phenomenon-in-the-making for two years before the public first viewed it in December 1997. It is predicted that when the numbers are in, it will go down in history as the biggest grossing movie of the twentieth century, and it is still amidst its initial release as of this writing. It also has the rare distinction of being the costliest cinematic adventure ever staged before a motion picture camera.

Writer / director / producer James Cameron didn't set out to make *Titanic* the most expensive film ever made—it just ended up

that way. In 1986 he directed the truly exciting science fiction masterpiece *Aliens*, which came in at $18 million. It seems downright cheap by comparison, but at the time that was considered a high-budget film. Then in 1991, with the special effects lavished on his *Terminator 2*, the film was produced for $93 million. Cameron topped himself when he directed *True Lies* in 1994, which cost $100 million. Now, with *Titanic* costing a record price of $200 million, it had to earn a reported $400 million just to break even. Fortunately for him, it has already topped the $600 million mark worldwide!

There were many risks from the very start of the film. First of all, coming in at three hours and fourteen minutes long, *Titanic* might have been seriously off-putting to mainstream audiences not used to sitting still in a theater for that long. Then there was the fact that the sinking of the *Titanic* had already been a black and white feature in the 1950s starring Barbara Stanwyck and Clifton Webb, and a concurrently running 1990s Broadway show. Could the market really bear such an epic film, when, in fact, the audience essentially already knew how the story ended? The ship sinks and nearly everyone

dies. To say the least, the whole project was one big gamble. Fortunately for everyone, including Leonardo DiCaprio, it has been a gamble that has paid off.

In James Cameron's vision, the story he wanted to film would be bookended by footage of the actual wreckage of the *Titanic*, filmed by a camera crew in a submarine. That alone ended up costing $4.5 million for those sequences. Then there was the matter of coming up with a *Titanic* ship to film. Should it be done with scale models and special effects? Instead, Cameron pushed for a nearly life-size model of the tragedy-bound ship. At 780 feet in length, the model he ended up with was built 90 percent to scale. Most of the film was shot on location at a huge facility in Rosarito Beach, Mexico.

Cameron had the model ship, the location, and the green light to start filming this cinematic dream of his. All he needed now was a box office-appealing cast. Oddly enough, playing the role of a romantic hero was about the last thing that DiCaprio was looking to do. And, James Cameron had his own reservations about casting him in the part as well. Leo had made a successful

Leonardo brought a scrappy exuberance to the role of Jack Dawson.

Kate Winslet as Rose to Leo's Jack. They were two souls thrown together by fate aboard the tragic luxury liner.

career out of playing misfits. Could he focus his acting talent towards being confident and appealing—as opposed to portraying a character who is as unappealing and maladjusted as possible?

In retrospect, James Cameron claims, "The curious thing is, I actually didn't want Leo at first. Leo was recommended by the studios, as were other young, hot actors . . . He didn't strike me as necessarily having the qualities that I wanted in Jack. But, I met him and basically just loved him. He can quickly charm a group of people without doing anything obvious . . . The second I met him I was convinced."

However, Leonardo's audition for the role of the appealing vagabond, Jack Dawson, almost ended in disaster. "He read it once, then started goofing around," Cameron reports, "and I could never get him to focus on it again. But for one split second, the shaft of light came down from the heavens and lit up the forest."

> *DiCaprio was paid his first film check for over $1 million for starring in Titanic.*

and once he was amidst filming, he found the role to be most appealing. "It was interesting because I've traditionally played characters that have been tortured in some aspect, whether it be by love, or drugs, or whatever, but this guy was like an open book," he explains. "He was an open-hearted guy with no demons, and it was more of a challenge than I ever thought it would be. I would like to be like that character. I mean, Jack sort of embodies a lot of things that I think we all find admirable. Like a bohemian that lives life day to day, finds his own sort of happiness. You try to be like that. I wish . . . I think I do have some of those aspects, but he's almost like the kind of guy we all wish to be."

One of the key elements to the success of the film is the fact that the on-screen chemistry between Leonardo DiCaprio and his leading lady, Kate Winslet, is so strong. When it was pointed out to Leo how well they interacted on screen, he enthusiastically agreed, saying, "I hope so. I mean, we have it in real life. I think she's such a terrific girl. It's unbelievable. We were such good friends throughout this whole movie. We were almost joined at the hip. Everything that we wanted to

The director did, however, lay down some ground rules to DiCaprio. "Look, I'm not going to make this guy brooding and neurotic. I not going to give him a tic and a limp and all the things you want," Cameron insisted.

Leonardo agreed to adhere to Cameron's vision, and all of a sudden he was signed to play the plum role of his career. In addition to the star stature that was to come with the assignment, if the film was a hit, was the fact that DiCaprio was paid his first film check for over $1 million for starring in *Titanic*.

The character of Jack Dawson represented a true departure for Leo,

complain about, we did it with each other, rather than doing it on the set and we got it all out in the open in our trailers. She's such a solid actress, and possesses so much strength on-screen, it's unbelievable. And I think she's gonna be one of our best!"

Describing the plot in the simplest terms possible, DiCaprio summed it up by saying, "It's a love story. Two people on a ship. And it deals a lot with different classes—a lower-class artist meeting this upper-class girl, and them falling in love. They define what's going on in their world. And all of a sudden, it all goes down."

Clearly, one of the reasons for the great success of the film *Titanic* is the fact that so many young girls and women are returning to the

theater time and time again to see Leonardo DiCaprio as this romantic character on the screen. As big as the phenomenon of this movie has grown, Leo has become to *Titanic* what Clark Gable is to *Gone With the Wind*. There is the same kind of sizzling sex appeal, combined with a role that is both romantic and strongly appealing.

The funny thing is that, suddenly, due to what the world has seen of Leo in *Titanic*, one would believe that he is quite a noble and classy character, and not at all the same kind of person who was seen urinating off of a table two years ago in *Total Eclipse*. Nor the foul-mouthed strung-out urban youth in *Basketball Diaries*. Nor the mischievous kid hitting actors over the head

with Twizzlers candies on the set of *William Shakespeare's Romeo + Juliet*.

Speaking of the two sides of Leo, Kate Winslet laughs, "He's probably the world's most beautiful-looking man, yet he doesn't think that he's gorgeous. And to me he's just smelly farty Leo."

The plot of *Titanic* is ingenious in that it involves the audience so heavily with the love story that is unfolding on this stunning luxury liner, and then all of a sudden, there's an iceberg. Instead of just becoming a special effects epic about the tragic sinking of the beloved ship, it is a well-crafted love story that just happens to have a fatal end for most of the characters. Then to top it all off—the sinking of the ship is so realistic and harrowing

Leo and Kate let loose with the passengers in the steerage section of the ship.

that it is impossible not to be swept up in the drama of it all.

The film begins with a modern day submarine trek to the bottom of the Atlantic Ocean to explore the remains of the H.M.S. *Titanic*, the most famous ship ever to sink. We are then introduced to one of the ship's handful of living survivors, fictional Rose DeWitt Bukater (Gloria Stuart). When she is brought down to see the ruins of the ship she escaped from all those years ago, she is prompted to retell the events that occurred on that very ship. Then the movie flashes back to 1912, and she tells the story of her voyage, the love affair she had on it, and of the *Titanic's* ultimate demise.

The story she tells is one about her encountering a young vagabond, Jack Dawson (Leonardo DiCaprio), aboard the *Titanic* on its maiden voyage. He had won the ticket only moments before, with a lucky hand in a dockside game of cards. Although ecstatic about boarding the ship, Jack soon finds that by possessing only a steerage class ticket, he is exempt from attending some of the ship's more glamorous events. He also has no idea how his life is about to change when he suddenly meets the young Rose (Kate Winslet).

Her mother, Ruth (Frances Fisher), is in the process of trying to marry Rose off to a spoiled rich cad by the name of Cal Hockley (Billy Zane), simply to tap into his family's bank account. So despondent is Rose that she attempts to kill herself by jumping off the back of the *Titanic*. She is instead rescued by a wandering stranger by the name of Jack Dawson.

As a reward for his act of heroism, Jack is asked to dine with the aristocracy that evening. He essentially steals the heart of Rose, who is now torn between two suitors: exciting but poor Jack who wants her heart, or rich male chauvinist Cal whom she can't stand. Love wins out, and Rose and Jack have a romantic affair on the ship that fateful night.

Not long afterward, when the

When the *Titanic* hit the iceberg, the love story swings into high gear.

fatal iceberg ruptures the underside of the ship, the love story is intensified by impending doom. Through a series of twisted circumstances, Jack is accused of theft, and is handcuffed to the pipes in a ship's office rooms down below. Since the ship is now sinking into the cold Atlantic, Rose has to heroically rescue her lover while the room fills with ice water. Their perils in the cold, cold waters of those flooded ship's corridors have already made cinematic history.

With all of the lifeboats now gone, and the rear section of the ship upended, we see the setting for one of the most touching farewell sequences ever recorded on film. When the movie cuts back to modern-day Rose, there is hardly a dry eye in the house. Tapping into everyone's emotions, the

film has gone to break one box office record after another.

The filming of the final half of *Titanic* was reportedly one physically challenging scene after another, especially for DiCaprio and Winslet. Those underwater sequences, when the ship is flooding, were especially difficult for the actors to do. How did Leo feel about having to film those scenes in the water time and time again? "It was cold!" he confirms. "There was a gigantic sort of tank that the interior of the *Titanic* was in, and it was on hydraulics. So it basically has the level of sea water to it and whenever he [James Cameron] wanted corridors to be flooded with sea water, he'd tip the hydraulics on it. And the water would come rushing in. It was always like a new

"I would like to be like that character. I mean, Jack sort of embodies a lot of things that I think we all find admirable. Like a bohemian that lives life day to day, finds his own sort of happiness."

sort of roller-coaster ride to jump into. Granted, after the fiftieth or sixtieth time doing it, it becomes tedious. But the initial excitement of doing it for the first time was cool."

The other scene that was tedious and terrifying to film was the one where the ship breaks in half and the back of the ship is suddenly hoisted up in the air. According to Leonardo, "It was hard to focus, it really was. I remember how they got one scene ready in about two hours, and all of a sudden I'm being, like, towed up on the back of a poop deck with a harness around my waist. There's, like, 200 extras cabled on with bungee cords, stuntmen ready to fall off and hit the cushioned girders. And then there's three cranes around us with huge spotlights. Kate and I just looked at each other like, 'How did we get here?'"

One of the most appealing aspects about seeing Leonardo in *Titanic* is to see how much more mature he appears on the screen. Only one year ago he looked like a young boy in *Marvin's Room*, and suddenly he looks like a young hunk. "I would agree that he does look older," says Kate Winslet. "But I don't think it's to do with the change in his face, but rather with a

Romancing the stone? This breathtaking sapphire necklace holds mystery aboard HMS *Titanic*.

These scenes aboard the sinking ship were amongst the most harrowing to film for Kate and Leonardo.

worldly wisdom he would probably hate to acknowledge he's acquired."

When *Titanic* opened in America, a week before Christmas 1997, it instantly hit number one in *Variety* magazine's box-office tally. The first week of its release, the week ending December 19, it brought in a reported 28.6 million dollars. By the week ending February 8, it was reportedly up to $312.6 million gross for America alone. It looks like it has a good shot at becoming the first ever one billion dollar-grossing movie!

Thanks to *Titanic,* and all of the press coverage he has had lavished on him, Leonardo is the movie world's most unanimously desirable young leading man. His fame has become a 1998 phenomenon of magazine cover stories and near daily reportage of his every move. But, will fame change rebellious Leo? Not likely. According to James Cameron, "Stardom may have captured his imagination for the moment, but I don't think it's where he started out, and I don't think it will be where he winds up. Leo wants to go the depths. The choices he's likely to make may disappoint people. He may not want to be Jack again for a while." For the time being, DiCaprio doesn't have to do anything more than follow his instincts, and be himself. The *Titanic* had sunk, but Leonardo DiCaprio soared.

Unmasking Leo's Talent

Leonardo at the premiere of *Titanic*, in Hollywood.

With *Titanic* the number one movie in America for over fourteen weeks, there suddenly was a Leonardo DiCaprio feeding frenzy. Everyone was rushing around trying to come up with sublicensing deals for him, movie offers, books, and magazines with

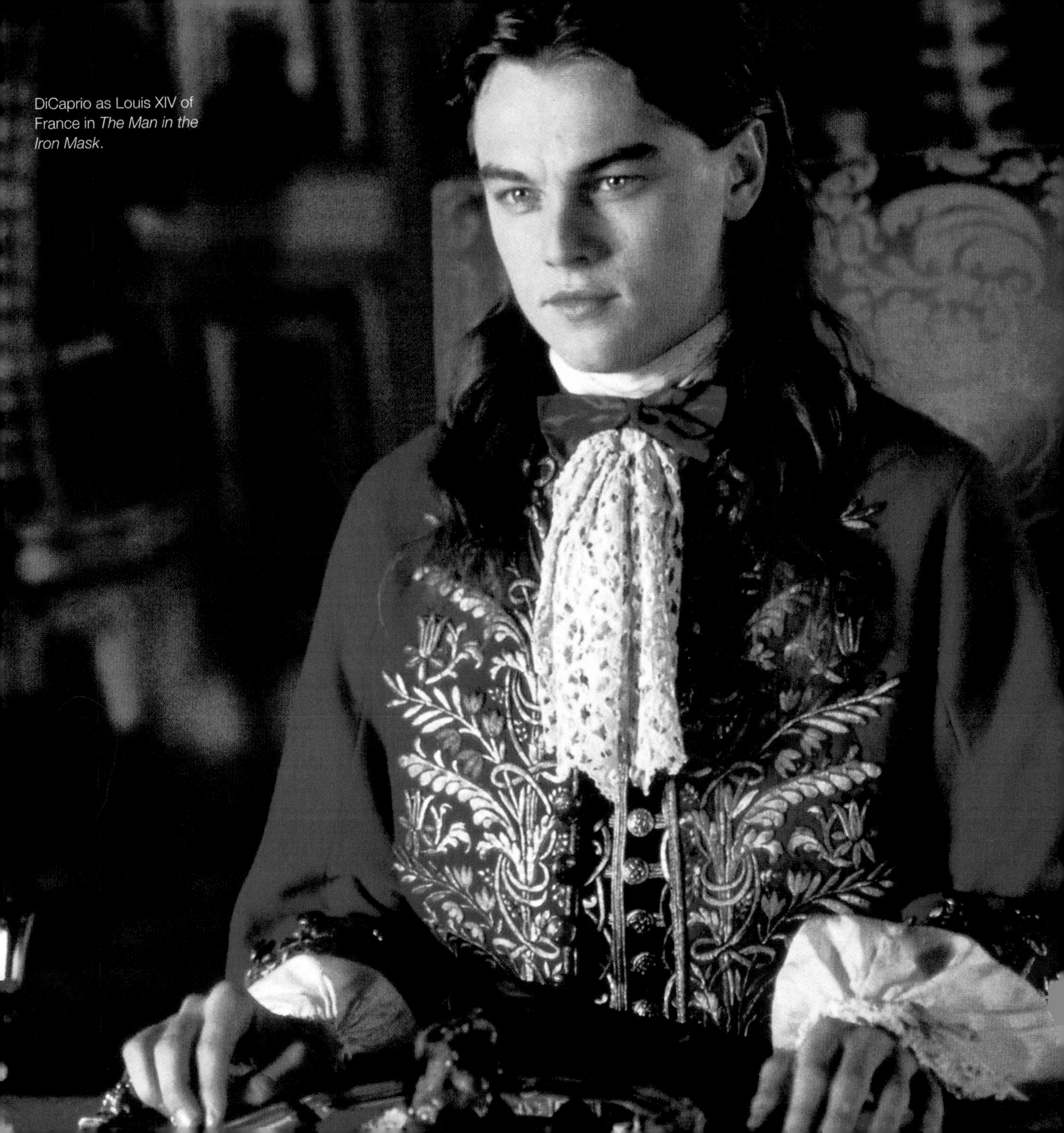

DiCaprio as Louis XIV of France in *The Man in the Iron Mask*.

his image emblazoned on them. Instead of capitalizing on any of the offers that have come his way, Leo has simply kept his focus on his career, and hanging out with his friends.

In January 1998 Leonardo was in the headlines when an aspiring filmmaker by the name of R. D. Robb surfaced, claiming that he had in his possession a new feature film starring Leonardo DiCaprio, called *Don's Plum*. News of the film came to light when Robb attempted to enter it in a couple of prestigious film festivals, but didn't have clearance from Leo.

Apparently, in 1995, when he was inbetween projects, a friend of his, R. D. Robb, came to Leonardo with a proposition. Robb was an aspiring director, and he had an idea for a short experimental film called *Don's Plum*. The script was mainly improvised, and it was about a bunch of people sitting in a diner complaining about their lot in life. It was never supposed to be anything but a short film, and kind of experimental at best. Once a shorter version of the film was finished, Robb decided that he liked it so much, he wanted to blow it up

Kate Winslet and Leonardo DiCaprio at the *Titanic* party following The Golden Globe Awards, January 19, 1998.

into a full film feature. When he approached Leonardo about making it into a longer film for public release, DiCaprio declined. In the wake of Leonardo's growing fame as a movie star, Robb pushed more and more to expand his film into a commercial vehicle. When *Titanic* became the blockbuster film of the decade, Robb became vocal about wanting *Don's Plum* to be seen in theaters. In early 1998 the producers of the film were still battling with Leonardo about getting him to sign a release form to allow the movie to be distributed. As of this writing, the project is still in limbo. According to the film's producer, David Stutman, "Leo liked this film, but for some reason he didn't want it seen."

Next came the announcement of the nominees for the 1998 Academy Awards. Much to everyone's delight, *Titanic* received nominations in fourteen categories. Kate Winslet was nominated for Best Actress, and Gloria Stuart was nominated for Best Supporting Actress. The big shock was that Leonardo DiCaprio was conspicuously missing from the Best Actor category. So shocked was the press that *The New York Daily News*

James Cameron displays one of his Golden Globe awards, which he won in the categories of Best Director and Best Film for *Titanic*. He is flanked by his two stars: Winslet and DiCaprio.

Thanks to Titanic *and all of the press coverage he has had lavished on him, Leonardo is the movie world's most unanimously desirable young leading man.*

Irmelin DiCaprio shakes hands with Britain's Prince Charles while her famous son looks on, at a special *Titanic* event

published as its headline on February 11, 1998: OSCAR SINKS HUNK—*14 nominations for "Titanic" tie Oscar record, but heartthrob Leonardo DiCaprio is snubbed.*

According to Jon Landau, James Cameron's coproducer, "Leo did a fantastic job. It's just unfortunate he came up against some really tough competition this year. But he is going to be a big star for years to come." The actors who were nominated in the category of Best Actor in 1998 were: Matt Damon for *Good Will Hunting*, Robert Duvall for *The Apostle*, Peter Fonda for *Ulee's Gold*, Dustin Hoffman for *Wag the Dog*, and Jack Nicholson for *As Good As It Gets.*

Knowing Leo, he was probably relieved not to have been nominated, so he wouldn't have to sweat it out at the Academy Awards, fearing that at any moment he could have to deliver an acceptance speech. In reality, Leonardo got bigger headlines by NOT getting nominated than those actors who did!

Spring 1998 saw the premiere of Leonardo DiCaprio's eleventh film release. As he explains, "I did a film over the summer [of 1997] called *The Man in the Iron Mask* with John Malkovich and Jeremy Irons and Gerard Depardieu and Gabriel Byrne and that was unbelievable, working with those guys. I mean it's so cool working with people in that caliber because they're so relaxed about everything. They're almost like children in a sense; it's fun for them at this point. And it was totally cool working on that. But for now, after that movie, I'm taking a long time off."

Since the completion of *The Man in the Iron Mask*, Leo has kept good his promise of taking a break from his acting career. He will next be seen in a cameo role as a celebrity in the next film directed by Woody Allen.

The biggest news in his personal life came when *People* magazine reported that he had finally moved out of his mother's house just before Christmas 1997. However, his ties to his parents still remain the closest in his life.

His father, George, keeps busy reading through potential scripts for his son. Says Leo, "My dad is a pretty hip dude, when it comes to old men. He reads a lot of scripts for me and eliminates some of them."

Speaking of her son's sudden screen success, his mother, Irmelin, exclaims, "I'm overwhelmed. I can't see him as other people do. All I'm concerned about is his health—sleep more, exercise more, eat better. That's the litany. The rest, I wouldn't care if he gave it up tomorrow."

As wild a reputation as Leonardo has, one might suspect that he has several body piercings and at least a couple of tattoos by now. However, he reports that with his liberal-thinking parents, there is nothing he could do that would shock them. "Whatever I did would be something they'd already done," he claims. "I mean, my dad would welcome it if I got a nose ring. I'm afraid of leaving a little hole in my face. Or having a tattoo and living with that stupid painting for the rest of my life. Why not just get a poster and put it up in your room?"

He credits his present day money sense to his less-than-advantaged childhood. Leo points to his humble beginnings and says, "You see where I come from, which is why the money they throw around doesn't get me. What would I need all that money for anyway? I'd be miserable in a mansion, all by myself. I don't want to sound like I'm some underprivileged kid, but you learn certain values. Like not accepting that because you're in a hotel you have to pay $5.00 for a Coke—just go down the block for a $3.00 six-pack! On the other hand,

Brooke Shields and Leonardo DiCaprio at one of 1998's Golden Globe parties.

I have a $600 leather jacket, and my $35,000 Jeep."

Instead of kowtowing to media-sponsored events, Leonardo prefers to hang out with his old friends. "I honestly don't know that many people in the business," he claims. "I mean, Lukas Haas is a good friend of mine, and I still talk to Juliette Lewis once in a while. But my main, real friends I've known for years. I don't need to have a lot of other friends around me. It's interesting—Toby McGuire, who's been my friend for a long time, is becoming successful right now. He's been doing a Woody Allen movie. He's a good guy."

So strong are his ties to his childhood friends that he has a special budget built into his location film contracts. That way, he has buddies he can hang out with when he isn't in front of the cameras.

Although he is in a position to get into writing or directing his own films, he is content to continue being an actor. "I think acting is enough for now. More than anything, I want to travel. And I know I want to really fall in love eventually," he says.

At the mention of marriage, Leonardo claims, "I don't know if

Leonardo romances Judith Godreche in *Man in the Iron Mask.*

John Malkovich and Leo in this exciting new version of the Alexandre Dumas literary classic.

I'm ever getting married. I'm probably not going to get married unless I live with somebody for ten or twenty years. But these people [Romeo and Juliet] took a chance and they did it. We don't have the balls that Romeo did."

When asked recently if fame had turned him into a girl magnet, he replied, "Girls don't really hit on me, no. I think if a girl wants to talk to me, she'll talk to somebody around me, but not me directly. I don't know what it is. They never really approach me."

Although he still cringes when he reads some of the things that are

written about him in the newspaper, he has come to a point where he just ignores it. "You know, I've just realized that—and this is the truth—no matter what happens, your work speaks for itself in the end. Some things I think aren't fair, but they're by no means out-and-out lies. Once you realize that nothing really matters, even some of the lies make your life more interesting sounding in the end!" he proclaims.

Leonardo's sights are so soundly on his career that he doesn't have time for romance at the moment. One thing that he is truly obsessed with is his intuition towards always

Leo and Kenneth Branagh in an upcoming and yet-untitled Woody Allen film. DiCaprio plays the role of a celebrity.

really charismatic, very perceptive and very charming." What impressed Mark Wahlberg the most about Leo is that "he's the most down-to-earth person I've met. Very un-Hollywood." His *Titanic* costar, Kate Winslet, sums it up best when she says, "Leo is absolutely awesome. No one can really get near him at this point."

One of the things that Leonardo DiCaprio is most happy about is his ability to consistently chose strong scripts. The last thing he wants to do at this point is have his career lose any of the momentum or any of the integrity that it has. He also doesn't want to lose himself in his career, or to alienate the people who are important to him. "It's important to direct where you want to go with it," he says. "The main thing for me is to just maintain my life with my family and friends. They treat me like Leo, not like 'Leonardo, Master Thespian.' That's all I need to maintain my sanity."

To keep it all in perspective, he tends to view it as a basketball game, as opposed to a boardroom operation. "It's sort of a five-on-five game: my publicists, my agents, my lawyers, my family, and me. I'm like the point guard, the one who

choosing film projects that are challenging and rewarding. He also only wants to be seen with actors of a certain stature. "I'm not saying I'm above the rest, or I'll only work with big costars, but I do have guidelines," he says. "There are people who have gotten good roles at my age, and their careers later slowly sloped down. Meaning no disrespect to anybody, but I want to avoid that by holding out for high quality projects. I've set a standard for myself, and hope I don't sell out and make stupid stuff."

So far, he has left a lasting impression on everyone he has worked with on the screen. According to Meryl Streep, "He's always compelling. You can't watch anything else when he's acting." His Juliet, Claire Danes, claims, "He's decides where the ball should be passed," he says.

One of the projects that has been predicted for him for quite some time is a biographical film about the life and premature death of actor James Dean. "I think it's going to happen," Leonardo says. "But the script has to be great. It could be a year. It could be never, but it would be really interesting to get inside an actor. I would be an actor playing an actor. It could be a little tricky. You can never really *BE* him. You're always imitating him."

One of the things that frustrates him the most is the way the press is constantly trying to compare him with other actors. He doesn't want to be "the next Johnny Depp," "the next River Phoenix," "the next James Dean," or the "next" anyone. He is happy to make his own decisions, and to define his own career with some of the most challenging and diverse roles around. "You get labeled," he claims. "But I want to be myself and act the way I act, not the way somebody else acts. I'll do my own thing and not try to be 'Hunk of the Month.'"

Whether by intention, by luck, by timing, or by fate, Leonardo DiCaprio has become known the

world over as the hottest young actor of 1998. Thanks to his portrayal of Jack Dawson in *Titanic*, there is nowhere on the globe where his name or image isn't known. Regardless of what he chooses as his next movie role, his fans can be assured that it could be just about anything: from a punk, to a desperado, to a tortured artist, to a misfit extraordinaire. He is rarely predictable with his choices, but, in whatever role he decides upon, he is always 100 percent connected to the

character. Whether he is playing a troubled youth like Hank in *Marvin's Room*, a defiant genius like Rimbaud in *Total Eclipse*, or Romeo in *William Shakespeare's Romeo + Juliet*, he puts everything he can into his work. Every new character he plays has a vibe and a passion all its own. Through each part he has portrayed on the screen, he has added a new dimension to his appeal as a screen star and to his craft as an actor. He is Leonardo DiCaprio: Romantic Hero.

Woody Allen (back to the camera) directs Leonardo DiCaprio in his performance.

Filmography

Critters 3 (1991)

CAST:

Aimee Brooks	Annie
John Calvin	Clifford
Katherine Cortez	Marcia
Leonardo DiCaprio	Josh
Geoffrey Blake	Frank

What's Eating Gilbert Grape?

Diana Bellamy	Rosalie
William Dennis Hunt	Briggs
Frances Bay	Mrs. Menges
Bill Zuckert	Mr. Menges
Don Opper	Charlie
Ugi	Terrance Mann

DIRECTOR	Kristine Peterson
PRODUCERS	Barry Opper
	Rupert Harvey
ASSOCIATE PRODUCER	Mark Ordesky
STORY BY	Rupert Harvey
SCREENPLAY	David J. Schow

Poison Ivy (1992)

CAST:

Tom Skerritt	Darryl Cooper
Sara Gilbert	"Cooper"
Drew Barrymore	Ivy
Cheryl Ladd	Georgie Cooper
Alan Stock	Bob

Jeanne Sakata	Isabelle
E. J. Moore	Kid
J. B. Quon	Another Kid
Leonardo DiCaprio	Guy
Michael Goldner	Man in Car
George Haynes	Dave
Daniel Gullahorn	Boy #2

DIRECTOR	Katt Shea Ruben
EXECUTIVE PRODUCERS	Peter Morgan
	Melissa Goddard
PRODUCERS	Andy Ruben
	Katt Shea Ruben
BASED ON A STORY BY	Peter Morgan
	Melissa Goddard
SCREENPLAY	Andy Ruben
	Katt Shea Ruben

This Boy's Life (1993)

CAST:

Robert DeNiro	Dwight
Ellen Barkin	Caroline
Leonardo DiCaprio	Toby

Jonah Blechman . . . . . *Arthur Gayle*
Eliza Dushku . . . . *Pearl*
Chris Cooper . . . . *Roy*
Carla Gugino . . . . *Norma*
Zack Ansley . . . . *Skipper*
Tracy Ellis . . . . *Kathy*
Kathy Kiney . . . . *Marion*
Bobby Zameroski . . . . . . *Arch Cook*
Tobey Maguire . . . . . . *Chuck Bolger*

DIRECTOR . . . Michael Caton-Jones
EXECUTIVE
PRODUCERS . . . . Peter Guber
Jon Peters
PRODUCER . . . . Art Linson
COPRODUCER . . . . Fitch Cady
BASED ON THE
BOOK BY . . . . Tobias Wolff
SCREENPLAY . . . . . Robert Getchell

What's Eating Gilbert Grape? (1993)

CAST:

Johnny Depp . . . . . . *Gilbert Grape*
Leonardo DiCaprio . . . *Arnie Grape*
Juliette Lewis . . . . *Beckie*
Mary Steenburgen . . . . *Betty Carver*
Darlene Cates . . . . *Mama*
Laura Harrington . . . . . *Amy Grape*
Mary Kate Schellhardt . . *Ellen Grape*
Kevin Tighe . . . . *Mr. Carver*
John C. Reilly . . . . *Tucker Van Dyke*
Crispin Glover . . . *Bobby McBurney*

Total Eclipse

Penelope
Branning . . . . *Becky's Grandma*
Tim Green . . . . *Mr. Lamson*
Susan Loughran . . . . . *Mrs. Lamson*
Rev. Robert B. Hedges . . . *Minister*
Mark Jordan . . . . *Todd Carver*
Cameron Pinley . . . . . *Doug Carver*
Brady Coleman . . . . . *Sheriff Farrel*
Tim Simek . . . . *Deputy*
Nicholas Stojanovich . . . . . . *Boy #1*
Libby Valleri . . . . *Waitress*
Kay Bower . . . . *Police Secretary*
Joe Stevens . . *Burger Barn Manager*
Mona Lee Pultz . . . . *Bakery Worker*

George Haynes . . . . *Dave*
Daniel Gullahorn . . . . *Boy #2*

DIRECTOR . . . . Lasse Halström
EXECUTIVE
PRODUCERS . . . . Lasse Halström
Alan C. Blomquist
PRODUCERS . . . . Bertil Ohlsson
David Matalon
Meir Teper
BASED ON THE
NOVEL BY . . . . Peter Hedges
SCREENPLAY . . . . Peter Hedges

Fay Masterson . . . . *Mattie Silk*
Raynor Scheine . . . . *Ratsy*
Woody Strode . . . *Charles Moonlight*
Jerry Swindall . . . . *Blind Boy*
Gary Sinise . . . . *Marshall*
Leonardo DiCaprio . . . . *Kid*

DIRECTOR . . . . Sam Raimi
EXECUTIVE PRODUCERS . . Toby Jaffe
Robert Tapert
PRODUCERS . . . . . . Joshua Donen
Allen Shapiro
Patrick Markey
WRITTEN BY . . . . . . Simon Moore

The Basketball Diaries (1995)

CAST:

Leonardo DiCaprio . . . . *Jim Carroll*
Lorraine Bracco . . . . . . *Jim's Mother*
Marilyn Sokol . . . *Chanting Woman*
James Madio . . . . *Pedro*
Patrick McGaw . . . . *Neutron*
Mark Wahlberg . . . . *Mickey*
Roy Cooper . . . . . . *Father McNelly*
Vinnie
Pastore . . . . . . *Construction Worker*
Bruno Kirby . . . . *Swifty*
Jimmy Papiris . . . . *Iggy*
Nick Gaetani . . . . *Referee #1*
Alexander Gaberman . . . . . . *Bobo*

Ben Jorgensen . . . . *Tommy*
Josh Mostel . . . . *Councilman*
Juliette Lewis . . . . *Diane Moody*
Michael Inperioli . . . . *Bobby*
Akiko Ashley . . . . *Stripper*
Ernie Hudson . . . . *Reggie*
Manny Alfaro . . . . *Manny*
Cynthia Daniel . . . . *Winkie*
Brittany Daniel . . . . *Blinkie*
Eric Betts . . . . *Drug Dealer #1*
Joyce R. Korbin . . . *Mugging Victim*
Barton Heyman . . *Confessional Priest*

Marvin's Room

The Quick and the Dead (1994)

CAST:

Sharon Stone . . . . . *Darryl Cooper*
Gene Hackman . . . . *Harod*
Russell Crowe . . . . *Cort*
Tobin Bell . . . . *Dog Kelly*
Roberts Blossom . . . . . *Doc Wallace*
Kevin Conway . . . . . . *Eugene Dred*
Keith David . . . . *Sgt. Cantrell*
Lance Henriksen . . . . . *Ace Handon*
Pat Hingle . . . *Horace the Bartender*
Olivia Burnette . . . . *Katie*
Mark Boone Junior . . . . *Sears*

DIRECTOR . . . . Scott Kalvert
EXECUTIVE
PRODUCERS . . . . . Chris Blackwell
                   Dan Genetti
PRODUCERS . . . . Liz Heller
            John Bard Mavulis
SCREENPLAY . . . . . Bryan Goluboff
BASED ON A
TRUE STORY BY . . . . Jim Carroll

DIRECTOR . . . . . Agnieszka Holland
EXECUTIVE
PRODUCERS . . . . . Jean-Yves Asselin
           Steffan Ahrenberg
           Pasquale Faubert
PRODUCER . . Jean Paul Ramsey Levi
COPRODUCERS . . Philip Hinchcliffe
                   Cat Villiers
SCREENPLAY . . Christopher Hampton

William Shakespeare's Romeo + Juliet (1996)

CAST:
Leonardo DiCaprio . . . . . . Romeo
Claire Danes . . . . Juliet
Jesse Bradford . . . . Balthazar
Vondie Curtis-Hall . . Captain Prince
Brian Denehy . . . . . Ted Montague
John Leguizamo . . . . Tybalt
Miriam Margolyes . . . . Nurse
Christina Pickles . . . . Caroline Montague

Total Eclipse (1995)

CAST:
Leonardo DiCaprio . . . . . . Arthur Rimbaud
David Thewlis . . . . . Paul Verlaine
Dominique Blanc . . . . Isabelle Rimbaud
Roman Bohringer . . . . . Mathilde Verlaine
Felicie Pasotti . . . . Cabarbaye
Nita Klein . . . . . Rimbaud's Mother
James Thieree . . . . Frederick
Emanuele Oppo . . . . Vitalle
Denise Chalem . . Mrs. Mauté de Fleurville
Andrzej Seweryn . . Mr. Mauté de Fleurville
Christoper Thompson . . . . . Carjat

Total Eclipse

Pete Postlethwaite . . Father Laurence
Paul Rudd. . . . . Dave Paris
Paul Scorvino. . . Felgencio Capulet
Diane Venora . . . . . Gloria Capulet
E. Emmet Walsh . . . . . Apothecary

DIRECTOR. . . . . . . Baz Luhrmann
EXECUTIVE
PRODUCERS . . . . Craig Pearce
                        Baz Luhrmann
PRODUCERS . . . Gabriella Martinelli
                        Baz Luhrmann

Marvin's Room (1996)

CAST:
Meryl Streep . . . . Lee
Leonardo DiCaprio . . . . Hank
Diane Keaton. . . . . Bessie
Robert DeNiro . . . . Dr. Wally
Hume Cronyn . . . . Marvin
Gwen Verdon . . . . Ruth
Hal Scardino . . . . Charlie
Dan Hendya. . . . . Bob
Cynthia Nixon . . . . Retirement
                        Home Director

DIRECTOR . . . . Jerry Zacks
EXECUTIVE
PRODUCERS . . . . . Tod Scott Brody
                        Lori Steinberg
COPRODUCERS. . . David Wisnievitz
                        Bonnie Palef
PRODUCERS. . . . . Scott Rudin
                        Jane Rosenthal
                        Robert DeNiro
SCREENPLAY. . . . . . Bryan Goluboff

Titanic (1997)

CAST:

Leonardo DiCaprio . . *Jack Dawson*
Kate Winslet . . *Rose DeWitt Bukater*
Billy Zane . . . . *Cal Hockley*
Gloria Stuart . . . . *Rose (present day)*
Kathy Bates . . . . *Molly Brown*
Bill Paxton . . . . *Brock Lovett*
Frances Fisher . *Ruth DeWitt Bukater*
Bernard Hill . . . . . *Capt E. J. Smith*
Jonathan Hyde . . . . . *J. Bruce Ismay*
David Warner . . . . . . *Spicer Lovejoy*
Victor Garber . . . . *Thomas Andrews*
Danny Nucci . . . . *Fabrizio DeRossi*
Suzy Amis . . . . *Lizzy Calvert*

DIRECTOR . . . . James Cameron
EXECUTIVE PRODUCER . Rae Sanchini
PRODUCERS . . . . . . James Cameron
Jon Laudau
SCREENPLAY . . . . . . James Cameron

The Man In the Iron Mask (1998)

CAST:

Leonardo DiCaprio . . . *French King Louis XIV*
Jeremy Irons . . . . *Aramis*
John Malkovich . . . . *Athos*
Gerard Depardieu . . . . *Porthos*

Gabriel Byrne . *Captain D'Artagnan*
Anne Parillaud . . . . . *Queen Mother, Anne of d'Autriche*
Judith Godreche . . . . *Christine*

DIRECTOR . . . . Randall Wallace
PRODUCERS . . . . . . Randall Wallace
Russ Smith
COPRODUCER . . . . . . René Dupont
SCREENPLAY . . . . . Randall Wallace
FROM THE
NOVEL BY . . . . . . Alexandre Dumas

Titanic

Video

1. CRITTERS 3 (1991)*
2. POISON IVY (1992)*
3. THIS BOY'S LIFE (1993)*
4. WHAT'S EATING GILBERT GRAPE? (1993)*
5. THE BASKETBALL DIARIES (1994)*
6. THE QUICK AND THE DEAD (1994)*
7. TOTAL ECLIPSE (1995)*
8. WILLIAM SHAKESPEARE'S ROMEO + JULIET (1996)*
9. MARVIN'S ROOM (1996)*
10. TITANIC (1997)
11. THE MAN IN THE IRON MASK (1998)

Video currently available

Educational Films

Mickey's Safety Club
How to Deal With a Parent Who Takes Drugs

TV Shows

Romper Room
Lassie
The Outsiders
Santa Barbara
Roseanne
Parenthood (one season) (1990)
Growing Pains (one season) (1991)

Leo has become to Titanic what Clark Gable is to Gone With the Wind.